A Short History of Cambridge University Press is an account of the world's oldest printing and publishing house, from its foundation in 1534 and its first publications in 1584, through to the present day. It emphasises the constitutional story of the Press, as an essential part of its parent university, and highlights the moments of crisis and change: Richard Bentley's revival in the 1690s, the Victorian renaissance in the 1850s, the rise of modern university publishing, two world wars, and the crisis of the 1970s, resolved by Geoffrey Cass's reconstruction. This history brings out the unique nature of the organisation, as both an educational charitable enterprise and a business operating throughout the whole world and now publishing over 1,400 titles a year.

Michael Black, the former University Publisher, is the author of several books, including the full-length history, *Cambridge University Press, 1584–1984.*

A SHORT HISTORY OF
CAMBRIDGE UNIVERSITY PRESS

A SHORT HISTORY OF
CAMBRIDGE
UNIVERSITY
PRESS

MICHAEL BLACK
FORMERLY UNIVERSITY PUBLISHER
AND FELLOW OF CLARE HALL, CAMBRIDGE

CAMBRIDGE
UNIVERSITY PRESS

Published by the Press Syndicate of the University of Cambridge
The Pitt Building, Trumpington Street, Cambridge CB2 1RP
40 West 20th Street, New York, NY 10011–4211, USA
10 Stamford Road, Oakleigh, Victoria 3166, Australia

© Cambridge University Press 1992

First published 1992

Printed in Great Britain at the University Press, Cambridge

A catalogue record for this book is available from the British Library

Library of Congress cataloguing in publication data

Black, Michael H.
A short history of Cambridge University Press/Michael Black.
p.   cm.
ISBN 0-521-42921-8 (pbk)
1. Cambridge University Press – History.   2. University presses –
England – Cambridge – History.   3. Scholarly publishing –
England – Cambridge – History.   4. Printing – England –
Cambridge – History.
1. Title.
Z232.C17B59   1991   070.5'94 – DC20   91-37492 CIP

ISBN 0 521 42921 8 paperback

UP

CONTENTS

vii

Illustrations are reproduced by kind permission of the Syndics of the University Library, the Keeper of the University Archives, and the Master and Fellows of Trinity College, Cambridge.
Photographs on pp. 74 and 75 are by Michael Manni Photographic; photographs on pp. 55, 83, 85, 94 and 95 are by Tim Rawle Associates.

INTRODUCTION

Cambridge University Press is both the oldest printing and publishing house in the world and the oldest university press. It is founded on a royal charter granted to the University in 1534 and has been operating continuously as a printing and publishing business since the first Cambridge book was printed in 1584. By the narrowest of margins it is older than the other great English university press, Oxford, which did not issue its first book until 1585.

It is in fact very hard for an ordinary firm, especially a family firm, to last for that kind of time. The family may die out; more probably the firm is taken over by another family or firm, or in modern times becomes part of a great industrial or commercial complex and in losing its independence loses much of its identity. Only if it is owned and run by a corporate entity which cannot itself be taken over in that way can it survive for hundreds of years, and there are not many such bodies.

The University of Cambridge is such a body. It was founded at the beginning of the thirteenth century. It is itself one of those independent charitable corporations, founded on an official charter which has the force of law, which are characteristically English. So old as to seem an indissoluble part of the fabric of English social life, they are none the less independent of the State, and self-governing. The University of Cambridge, like its constituent colleges, exists and uses its funds entirely in order to exercise its scholarly functions, which are traditionally expressed as 'education, religion, learning and research'. University and colleges together are like a federation of charitable trusts acting in concert with each other. Though they receive funds from central government, they also have their own endowment and income and these are devoted entirely to the acquisition, conservation and dissemination of knowledge, to the education of students within the walls of the university itself, and to the spreading of knowledge in the wider world.

Clearly, institutions or facilities which have the aim of conserving knowledge (as in libraries) or conveying it (by printing and publishing) are crucial to those functions. A university is still primarily a place where books are used and written. An ancient university had from its very beginning to make provision for their supply.

THE FIRST STATIONERS

Before the invention of printing, books were handwritten in single copies and were scarce and valuable commodities. These manuscripts for hundreds of years supported a number of trades: parchment- and papermakers, inkmakers, the scribes themselves, bookbinders, and the middlemen who traded in them. These last were called stationers, a term which survives. Many stationers sold new and second-hand manuscript books, and, to make ends meet, also engaged in one of the productive skills themselves. Often they were bookbinders, since manuscripts and later printed books were usually transported unbound to the place of sale and then bound to suit the taste of the purchaser.

Apart from the great centres of population such as capital cities, stationers were most likely to be found in places of learning, especially the university towns. The university found itself regulating this in the same way as other trades, so that the interests of its members were protected. It appointed its own official stationers, who had recognised status and functions, wore a special academic gown and attended certain ceremonies. In particular they were valuers of books as well as suppliers. In days when a book was a major item of expenditure, books could be used as pledges or guarantees of a loan; poor students would often deposit a book as a 'caution' in this way and the stationers would supervise the transaction. Apart from that, they were responsible for copying, binding, stocking and selling the books that the libraries, teachers and students needed.

From medieval times, members of trades and professions have had their associations. In England there still exist ancient guilds, especially in the City of London. These are the descendants of the old trade guilds which regulated entry to a craft or trade, supervised apprenticeship, recognised the transition to the higher grades of freeman and master, acted to some extent as provident societies for members who had fallen on bad times, and in general protected the interests of members. In modern terms, they were something between a trade union, an employers' association and a lobby for a specific interest. Stationers in the University of Cambridge would have been members of two corporate bodies, university and guild: the possibility of tension or conflict between them is an important element of this story.

Printing was invented in Germany in the 1450s. It spread relatively quickly into Switzerland, North Italy, the Low Countries and France and printed books began to be a part of international trade. But for a generation or two printing was a European skill and printed books an import trade. Caxton set up his press in London in 1476 and slowly an English trade in printed books began, centred in London, especially in the bookselling area round St Paul's Cathedral.

In Cambridge too the stationers had their bookselling area. As it is today, the old street we call Trinity Street, then called the High Street, was their centre, especially the area where it passed the University Church, St Mary the Great. Here opposite the Old Schools, the teaching and examining centre, was the best place to attract trade. Great St Mary's was almost the stationers' church: a number of them were churchwardens, and some were buried there. As at St Paul's in London, it was also possible to set up a stall in the churchyard, or even against the church wall, and trade there, though stationers and printers also worked from permanent premises in the High Street and nearby.

The Cambridge Stationers included a noticeable number of Europeans from the Low Countries and three in particular play an important part in this story in the early 1500s. Garret Godfrey, Nicholas Speryng, and Segar Nicolson all came from the Netherlands. They were what was called 'denizens', that is, foreigners with a right to settle and trade alongside native citizens. Nicolson was younger than the others, may have been a second-generation denizen, had been a student at Gonville Hall, now Gonville and Caius College, and like many members of that college was what later was called a Protestant. All three must have been aware of the reforming movement in Germany, and Godfrey and Speryng also knew the great scholar and writer Erasmus, who came to Cambridge in 1511–14. That was before the new ideas became open revolt, but already contacts through the book-trades with European thinkers had a tinge of the forbidden. The most direct route for trade was by sea: the great European ports at the mouths of the Rhine and Scheldt opened the way by river and sea from the heart of Germany to England by the East coast ports; indeed you could sail right through to Cambridge. So it was possible, but dangerous, to import the books of reforming thinkers.

Luther nailed his theses to the door of the church in Wittenberg in 1517, was excommunicated in 1520, and published his German translation of the New Testament in 1522, inaugurating a century or more of strife. In the intellectual struggle the new art of printing was a crucial instrument. The freedom to publish, as against the desire of all the contesting parties to control what was published in their own territories, became literally a burning issue: Nicolson went to prison for his beliefs, and later saw a friend burnt on Jesus Green. There was in Cambridge in the 1520s a small Protestant group of advanced thinkers, to which he belonged. But the University authorities were traditionally orthodox, suspicious of new thinking, and prepared to be repressive. For a time, it must have been difficult to distinguish between the scholarly innovators, like Erasmus, who wanted to reform scholarship, and the more radical people who wanted to reform the whole Church.

Just at the moment when the old world was about to dissolve in conflict, the first printer arrived in Cambridge. John Lair of Siegburg in Germany was known in Cambridge as John Siberch. He was known to Erasmus and to the Cambridge humanist scholars and came to Cambridge in 1520 to set up a small press. He was given a loan by the University and it is likely that he was accepted as a Stationer, simply differing from the others in that his specialism was printing. He produced ten books in the new roman types – a sign of humanist sympathies. More traditional books went on being set in the old 'gothic' or blackletter type for the rest of the century, and Siberch himself used blackletter for the little 'selling lines' he printed in English. He lived and worked in a tenement called 'The King's Arms' in a long-since demolished street where the Trinity Street range of Gonville and Caius now stands. He probably had one press and a single apprentice, doing most of the work himself. He had a small amount of Greek type, and so called himself 'the first printer in both languages in England'. (The two languages were Latin, the international language of the educated, and Greek, the language of the new humanist scholarship.) He left in 1523 and went back to Germany, probably because he found he could not make a living as a printer in Cambridge. This would have been because the local sale was not enough to support him, and the London stationers would not have been pleased to face competition from a newcomer and a foreigner. And indeed legislation was passed at that time to restrict the entry of foreigners into the English booktrades; it was beginning to be felt that the national economic interest must be protected, and a national industry built up.

THE CHARTER

After this brief start or false dawn there was no printing in Cambridge until 1584 – a long gap. But the University took an absolutely crucial step to establish its right to be, when it chose, a centre of printing and publishing. In 1529 it petitioned the Lord Chancellor to formalise its traditional right to appoint its own stationers, and in 1534 Cambridge received from the king Letters Patent (in other words, a royal charter) recognising that right. The Letters Patent are the essential foundation of the University's printing and publishing tradition, and were the key document in all its later

Henry VIII's Letters Patent of 1534. Although it was written on vellum, which is very durable, the document, now in the University Archives, has deteriorated over the years; but the fine initial with the king's portrait inside it and the large first line of script are still clearly discernible.

disputes with other authorities, and in its own recurrent examinations of its role.

Because of its importance, the whole document, in English translation, is given at the end of this book. The substantive points may be summarised: there were to be three stationers *or printers*; they could print 'all manner of books'; they could sell them wherever they chose; the only licensing or censoring authority they had to recognise was that of the University itself, exercised by the Vice-Chancellor and three doctors. In effect, the University was being recognised as independent of any attempted control by other authorities.

Not surprisingly, Godfrey, Speryng and Nicolson were duly appointed the three Stationers to the University. The office went on being filled from now on until the alternative 'or printer' was adopted in 1583, and the office of University Printer has been held ever since.

Some years before this happened, the London guild of Stationers also formalised its status. In 1557 it became, by similar royal charter, the Stationers' Company. It was given the right to restrict entry into the bookselling, printing and other book-trades, which were to be concentrated in London, and to control publication by maintaining a register in which all new publications had to be entered. From the point of view of the central authority this was a way of securing political control by centralising the trade and making it self-policing for fear of losing its privileges. At once, the stage was set for conflict with anyone outside London who attempted to set up a press and operate it independently. At much the same time some of the London printers were beginning to operate like publishers, for instance by commissioning printing from those who were willing to remain sub-contractors or had not the capital to do anything else. Another important tactic was to acquire the monopoly (what we should now call the copyright) in a particular title that sold well or – more threatening to the interests of others – to have a monopoly in a whole category of books. In particular, the right to print and sell the English Bible – the best seller of all – was beginning to be concentrated in a few hands. First of all, it was a matter of the right to print in certain formats, but after 1577 the then Royal Printer Christopher Barker acquired a royal patent which seemed to give him and his heirs and assigns the sole right to print all Bibles in English.

THE FIRST CAMBRIDGE PRESS

When the University decided that it would at last exercise its right to appoint its own printer, it knew that it would have a fight on its hands. Documents still survive which indicate that in 1583 it was securing its position by writing to influential statesmen who could be counted on to back their old University. In that year, on 3 May, a Grace was passed appointing Thomas Thomas University Printer. (A Grace is a proposal presented to the Senate, the University's controlling assembly, asking for a favouring vote.) Translated, the record states:

It was agreed that *Magister* Thomas [i.e. Thomas was an MA of the University] should be one of your three printers of books with all the privileges assigned to those printers...

It is clear that the Charter had been consulted, and the University was being careful to invoke its terms. Thomas sent to London for his equipment, only to find that it had been impounded by the Stationers, who had become aware of what was intended, and meant to assert *their* rights. The University went into action, called on the aid of its powerful friends with well-considered letters, and the press and types were released. Here was a victory over the Stationers, but it was only the first skirmish in a long war. Thomas issued his first books in 1584, and ever since that date there has been continuous printing and publishing in Cambridge. The very first Cambridge book was *Two Treatises of the Lord's Holy Supper*.

Thomas Thomas, the first Cambridge Printer, was born in 1553 and went to Eton and on to King's College, where he became a Fellow. He married the widow of a stationer–bookbinder, and carried on the business. He was a Latin scholar of ability and a very pious man with Presbyterian sympathies. Some of the books he printed furthered the religious cause, but he also edited a Latin text. His most famous and successful publication was a Latin dictionary which he had revised and edited himself and which went on being reprinted in the next century. He was only thirty-five when he died, having been Printer for five years. His successor John Legate wrote this tribute to him in the eleventh edition of the Dictionary:

He was about 30 years ago a famous Printer among your Cantabrigians; yes, something more than a printer such as we now are, who understand the Latin that we print no more than Bellerophon the letters that he carried, and who sell in our shops

TWO TREATISES
OF THE LORD HIS
HOLIE SVPPER:

THE ONE INSTRVCTING THE
SERVANTS OF GOD HOW THEY
ſhould be prepared when they come to the
holy Supper of our onely Sauiour
Ieſus Chriſt:

*Whereunto is annexed a Dialogue conteining the principall
points neceſſarie to be knowne and vnderſtood of all them
that are to be partakers of the holy Supper:*

The other ſetting forth Dialoguewiſe the whole vſe of
the Supper: Whereunto alſo is adioyned a briefe
and learned treatiſe of the true Sacrifice and true
Prieſt.

*Written in the French tongue by Yues Rouſſeau and Iohn de
l'Eſpine Miniſters of the word of God, and latelie tranſla-
ted into Engliſh.*

I. CORINTH. II. 28. Let a man examine himſelfe, and ſo let
him eate of this bread, and drinke of this cup.

IOHN 6. 58.   This is the bread which came downe from
heauen: not as your fathers haue eaten Manna, and are dead.
He that eateth of this bread, ſhall liue for euer.

PSAL. 51. 16.   Thou deſireſt no ſacrifice, though we would
giue it: thou deliteſt not in burnt offering. The ſacrifices of
God are a contrite ſpirit: a contrite and broken heart, O God,
thou wilt not deſpiſe.

Imprinted by Thomas Thomas Printer to the
Vniuerſitie of Cambridge.
1584.

Title-pages of books printed by Thomas Thomas.
(a) Thomas's first book: the *Two Treatises*, 1584.

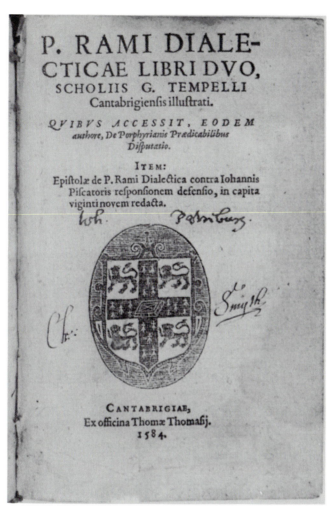

P. RAMI DIALE-
CTICAE LIBRI DVO,
SCHOLIIS G. TEMPELLI
Cantabrigienſis illuſtrati.

QVIBVS ACCESSIT, EODEM
authore, De Porphyrianis Prædicabilibus
Diſputatio.

ITEM:
Epiſtolæ de P. Rami Dialectica contra Iohannis
Piſcatoris reſponſionem defenſio, in capita
viginti novem redacta.

CANTABRIGIAE,
Ex officina Thomæ Thomaſij.
1584.

(b) Pierre de la Ramée's *Dialectic*, a popular textbook with an undergraduate
sale. Note the use of the University's coat of arms as an imprint. The arms
had been granted to the University in 1573. Thomas used the same block on
some of his bindings.

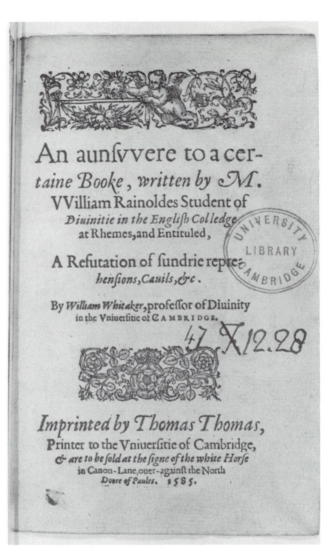

(c) William Whitaker's *An Answer to a Certain Book*, 1585. Whitaker, Professor of Divinity, was a fierce Calvinist, and very polemical. This answer to a Roman Catholic attack on the English Church shows where Thomas's own sympathies lay.

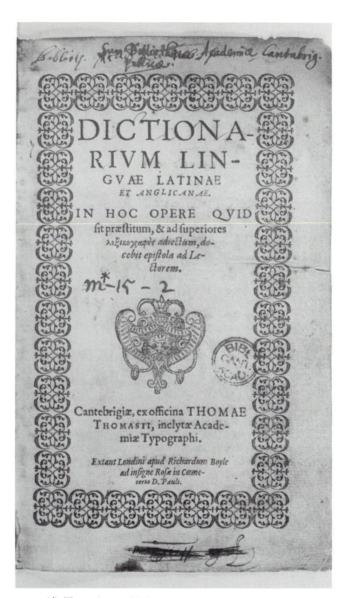

DICTIONA-
RIVM LIN-
GVÆ LATINAE
ET ANGLICANAE.

IN HOC OPERE QVID
fit præftitum, & ad fuperiores
λεξικογραφος adiectum, do-
cebit epiftola ad Le-
ctorem.

Cantebrigiæ, ex officina THOMAE
THOMASII, inclytæ Acade-
miæ Typographi.

Extant Londini apud Richardum Boyle
ad infigne Rofæ in Cœme-
terio D. Pauli.

(d) Thomas's own Dictionary of the Latin Language, 1587.

nothing of our own except the paper 'black with the press's sweat'. But he, a companion of the Stephenses [the Estiennes, the great dynasty of French scholar printers] and the other, very few printers of the true kind and best omen, was of the opinion that it was men of learning, thoroughly imbued with academic studies, who should give themselves to cultivating and rightly employing that illustrious benefit sent down from heaven and given to aid mankind and perpetuate the arts.

Thomas had one press, perhaps two or three apprentices, and worked in his shop in the Regent Walk, immediately opposite the West door of Great St Mary's. He was buried in the churchyard in 1588 and was succeeded by Legate.

Legate himself established an important precedent: he printed a New Testament in 1590 and then the first Cambridge Bible in 1591. It was a small octavo edition of the very popular Geneva Bible, in roman type. This at once sparked off another conflict with the London Stationers, and especially with Barker, who claimed that all Bibles were his monopoly. The University, going back to the words of the charter, relied on the fact that their Printer was entitled to print 'all manner of books' – and that must include Bibles. In a long letter to Lord Burghley, who as Lord High Treasurer was the chief minister under Elizabeth, and who was also Chancellor of the University and had intervened on its behalf when the dispute arose over Thomas's appointment, the University now appealed to the validity of its own charter, which pre-dated the other charters, the Stationers', and Barker's. They did not question other people's rights;

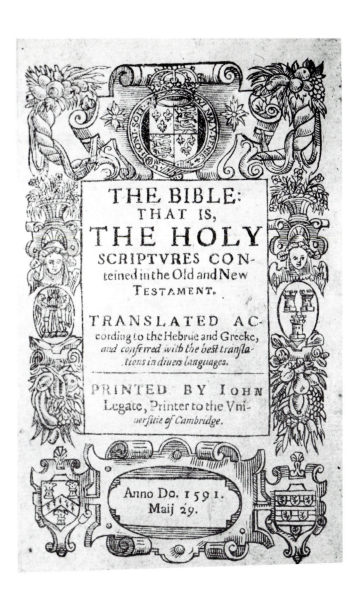

THE BIBLE:
THAT IS,
THE HOLY
SCRIPTVRES CON-
teined in the Old and New
TESTAMENT.

TRANSLATED AC-
cording to the Hebrue and Greeke,
and conferred with the best translations in diuers languages.

PRINTED BY IOHN
Legate, Printer to the Vniuersitie of Cambridge.

Anno Do. 1591.
Maij 29.

Early Bibles.
(a) The first Bible, 1591. Legate's little octavo Bible gave the Geneva
Version, then the preferred version of puritan readers, in roman type, and
so was readable and handy.

(b) The first Cambridge KJV, 1629. The so-called Authorised, or King James Version of 1611 was at first printed in blackletter in a large format in London only. The first Cambridge edition was more accurate and cheaper than the current London editions.

THE HOLY
BIBLE
CONTAINING THE
OLD TESTAMENT
AND THE NEW:

Newly translated out of the originall Tongues, and with the former translations diligently compared and revised, by his Majesties speciall command.

Appointed to be read in
CHURCHES.

Printed by Tho: Buck, and Roger Daniel, Printers to the University of Cambridge.

(c) The Buck and Daniel folio, 1638.

they simply insisted on their own. It seems that they won, and the dispute died down until the 1620s. Meanwhile Legate married the daughter of Barker, and became Master of the Stationers' Company in 1604, having left Cambridge in 1601. He kept the title of Printer, but was effectively succeeded by Cantrell Legge in 1606.

CONFLICT WITH THE STATIONERS

So the Cambridge Press had been set up against opposition and had survived the first years. The University had demonstrated a firm will to exercise its right to have its printers, and not to give up when the going was rough. None the less, its history during the seventeenth century is a record of the continuing fight with the Stationers' Company.

There were moments when outright struggle burst out again: for instance when Cambridge printed its first edition of the King James Bible in 1629. By this time the new Bible of 1611 was being recognised as the authoritative Bible of English-speakers. It had been treated by Barker as very much his own, since he had printed (rather hastily and inaccurately) the first edition, and he had, to do him justice, defrayed some of the costs of publication. But Cambridge had been cultivating a relationship with Charles I, had been granted a new charter by him in 1628, and no doubt felt emboldened to take on the London monopolists: all the more so in that two or three of the original translators still lived in Cambridge, and were able to help to make the new edition more consistent and accurate. It was thus possible to present the new Cambridge Bible as a distinct improvement on the London editions.

But there were also moments when both sides tried to find ways of living together. Legate showed such a way, by marrying into the opposition, and then by winning supreme status within the London Company. At times both the Cambridge and the London antagonists were capable of thinking 'We are all Stationers. Why are we fighting? Can't we find a way of living together?' and often they did; but increasingly this became a matter of Cambridge being willing to compromise. It could be in a relatively small matter, such as being prepared, for an annual payment, not to print certain books which were a London monopoly. A variant of that arrangement was that Cambridge would agree to print certain books, but at the request of the Londoners, supplying them with the whole edition at a special price. It is clear that both of these arrangements subtly undermined Cambridge's independence. Still more compromising were those times when the Cambridge right was effectively 'farmed' by the Stationers, who put in their nominee as Printer. The Stationers themselves went through a difficult time during the Commonwealth period; with no monarch, there could be no royal printer, and all the previous legislation about publication lapsed or was in question. But Cromwell in 1656 conferred the Bible privilege on Henry Hills and John Field. Field himself had in 1655 become Printer to the University, so that in this way the government of the time had both

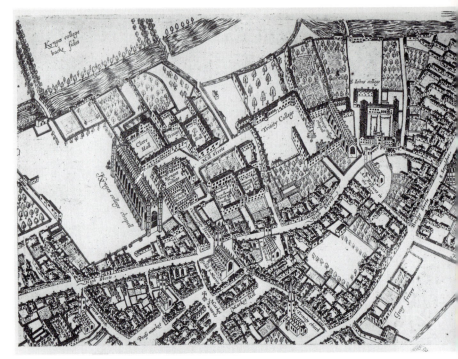

Hamond's map of Cambridge. Hamond's very large plan, 1592, shows in
detail the contemporary layout of Cambridge's streets. The old High Street
is now Trinity Street and King's Parade. Note the houses in front of King's
Chapel; and University Street, where the Senate House now stands,
between the Old Schools and Great St Mary's. Market Square was then
much smaller, with houses on much of the present open space. Siberch lived
and worked where the nineteenth-century building of Caius now faces the
old bookshop on the corner site. Thomas Thomas worked in University
Street, directly opposite Great St Mary's. In the seventeenth century the
University Printing House moved into the Market Hill area; one site being
next to the old Rose Inn on the North side; one 'at the South side of the
Steeple of Great St Mary's'; one where Rose Crescent joins Market Hill.
Thomas Buck used the old building which had once been the refectory of
the former Augustinian Friary in Free School Lane (cf. the modern Friar
House nearby). John Hayes moved the Press to Queens' Lane, where it
stayed until it moved into the Old Press site behind the Pitt Building.

the London and the Cambridge printers controlled by Parliament men, while Field had a comfortable monopoly.

What is more, Field survived the restoration of the monarchy. He was Printer until 1669, when he was succeeded by John Hayes. Field had moved the Printing House to the corner of Queens' Lane, where the garden of the Master's Lodge of St Catharine's College now lies, and it was to remain there until early in the nineteenth century.

Field was at the least on good terms, the University thought on too good terms, with the Stationers. Hayes was appointed on the understanding that there were to be no more arrangements with London. He remained in office until 1705, but in fact during his time the deals became secret and had a whiff of corruption about them. It was, one may suspect, disappointment or even disgust with this way of operating the University's privilege that led a small group of eminent men to propose a reform. This led to Richard Bentley's 'Public Press' – 'public' here being used in its old sense, meaning not owned by an individual college or a private person, and therefore being like what we should now call a University Press: in the same way what is now the University Library was for centuries called the Public Library. But before turning to Bentley, it makes sense to sum up the whole enterprise so far.

The Press had now survived for a century and this long survival had elements of victory and of defeat. It constituted victory for the Press, because both political and trading difficulties and dangers had been overcome. In 1584 Cambridge had wanted a press because the Puritan members of the University wished to be able to publish their books, or books which advanced their cause, without being subject to the control of moderate churchmen in London. Then, during the Civil War, writers and printers ran the risk of offending both sides and Cambridge itself was purged of royalist dons when Parliament won. At one moment both the Printer and the Vice-Chancellor were called before Parliament to explain an offending publication. When finally the monarchy was restored, civil peace meant a return to the old trouble with the Stationers, who finally attained such an influence over the printing of popular lines which were needed to enable the Press to survive that the University was bound to ask whether its rights were being used on its own behalf or that of others.

For the Stationers there were elements of defeat as well. They had not been able to suppress printing at Cambridge in 1584 or since. In lawsuits the Cambridge charters of 1534 and 1628 had been recognised as having as much validity as the Stationers' charter of 1577 or Barker's Bible privilege. What they had been able to do was to exercise their greater economic power, and consistently to squeeze the Cambridge printers by market pressures. In the end they had been able to ensure that the Cambridge patent was often held by people who were members of their own Company, or friends, or timid people who did not want a war. Powerful London printers were able to treat Cambridge as one of their suppliers of schoolbooks or almanacs or Bibles and Prayer books. They

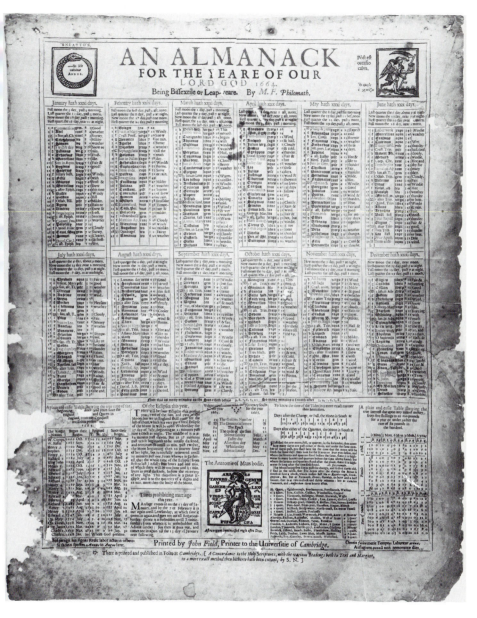

An almanac. This is a broadsheet almanac, which could be pinned to the wall as a calendar. Almanacs were also printed as little books.

did not mind if the printer also did a little work for the University: learned works with a small sale were no threat.

All this time the Press consisted of a single master-printer, a few journeymen and an apprentice or two, in a small workshop in the centre of Cambridge. It was like any other small printing house except that the Printer had entered into an agreement with the University which had become a traditional arrangement with a hundred years of history. Like Thomas Thomas, he had been appointed, and his appointment confirmed, by Grace of the University's Senate. He had made a formal undertaking not to print heretical or treasonous matter, and had undertaken to pay the University a certain sum each year for his office. He had to recover this from his printing and bookselling, as well as paying the rent of his house, buying and replacing his equipment, and paying his men. The University at this time owned neither the shop nor the presses and types. But he knew that if he were in trouble with the Stationers, the University would back him. To make sure that in any dispute it could be shown that the terms of the Charter had been implemented, he would keep a file of copies of title-pages, signed by the Vice-Chancellor and three doctors. For the internal purposes of University administration, he would print certain documents and notices. When royal persons were born, married or died, he would print a little volume of congratulatory verses in Latin, in which the Cambridge poets displayed their skill and brought themselves to the attention of the great. He would print sermons by preachers to the University. From time to

AB ECCLESIASTICO IVDICE
arbitrante in commiſſione adminiſtrationis
bonorum ab inteſtato decedentium non licet appellare. Arg. ti. ff. de le. dd.
& can. de accuſ. ſuper his.

Quid te conquereris Ieſum? quid iudice ſanéto
  Diſceptante, nona lite moleſtus ades.
Define puſtitia ſacrum turbare ſenatum
  Define vindictam quærere quiſquis eris.
Tu nullis tabulis inſcripſit dextra paterna
  Hæredem, rebus quo fruerere, ſuum.
Perfunétus fato pater eſt, nec quem cupit uti
  Ipſe bonis parvis, chartula parva docet.
Has ſacroſanétus iudex componere lites
  Nemo alius debet, voce quieſce, decet.
Hoc ſtatuit rex Henricus, qui nominis eius
  Oétavius nobis integra iura dedit.
Si quem defunétum vel bina prole parentem,
  Mors gravis abripiens in cava buſta trahet;
Qui tabulas nullas ſcripſit, nullumq; reliquit
  Hæredis certi nomen, uterq; petat.
Iudicis hoc ſacri eſt minus, dicatur & hæres,
  Et bona poſſideat quem iubet ille patris.
Nominet indignum, fac cauſſa nominet auri,
  Nullus erit. cuius q uerere poſſit opem.
Sæd ſolet: in rebus modicis ubi damna putantur
  Parva, modus nobis iſte tenendus erit,
Fortia concordis ſerventur vincula pacis,
  Creſcat amor verus, non violanda fides.
Da de iure tuo, minor eſt iaétura carere
  Quod modicum eſt, pacem quàm violare bonam.
Hoc debes patriæ, reſpublica poſtulat, inter
  Concives flagrans ut teneatur amor.

ERGO.

Defunéto domino, nec declarante ſuarum
  Hæredem rerum quem poſiturus erat.
Sanétior hæredem iudex pro iure creabit
  Quolibet inuito, iudiciumq; ratum eſt.
Gnoſiacum appelles Minoa, nec ille iuvare
  Iudice ſacro diſcutiente volet.

SOLA POENITENTIA INFIR-
matur teſtamentum. Arg. q. ſi hæres.
ff. ſi tabulæ teſtamenti nulla
extabunt.

Eſt teſtamenti faciundi formula priſca
  Solennis, tali conſtabilita modo.
Ut ſine ſeptenis non fiat teſtibus, hæres
  Ut non impellat, ſollicitetve patrem.
Languida membra licet mens ut non ægra gubernet,
  Ut teſtes propria ſignet & ille manu.
Si tamen iſtius ſolvuntur vincla ſigilli,
  Qui faciet, minor eſt, irrita cunéta, labor.
Aſpicis ut longo, quæ tempore creverat, ulmum
  Excindat venti vis violenta ſtatim.
Erigit in multos excelſa palatia princeps
  Annos, quæ famæ ſtent monumenta ſua.
Cùm ruit, hæc uno balliſtæ diſiicit iétu
  Miles, quæ multo condidit ille die.
Contrahitur ſubito morbus, depellitur ægrè,
  Qua perit, haud ipſa quæritur arte ſalui.
Ut valeas, viétu tenui medico q, perito
  Utendum, ſolus tu tibi cauſa mali.
Sic teſtamentum qui fecit ritibus uſus
  Multis, id proprio ſolvere iure poteſt.
Siq; prius ſtudium iam depoſuiſſe videntur
  Hæredes, domini feraq; fata putent.
Scripſerit ipſe novos, rerum potientur, & illud
  Infirmas ſcriptum, pænituiſſe ſui.

ERGO.

Non, in quas blando tabulas irrepſeris, ore,
  Ante obitum domini, dixeris eſſe ratas.
Auferet id ſolus tibi, quod non detulit ille
  Solus, quodq; tuum iam fuit. eius erit.

CANTABRIGIÆ EX Officina THOMÆ THOMASII. Iulij. 5. 1585.

Jobbing for the University: Tripos verses. Until the eighteenth century, the Tripos Examination was entirely oral, conducted in public, and had an element of spectacle. Tripos verses were handed out to senior members and distinguished visitors, and took the form of an elegant comment in Latin verse on the sort of topic being examined. This broadsheet is the ancestor of all University official printing, and jobbing for the Colleges and societies.

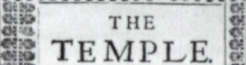

THE
TEMPLE.

SACRED POEMS
AND
PRIVATE EJA-
CULATIONS.

By Mr. George Herbert.

Psal. 29.
In his Temple doth every
man speak of his honour.

CAMBRIDGE:
Printed by *Thom. Buck,*
and *Roger Daniel,* printers
to the Universitie.
1633.

¶ Easter wings.

Lord, who createdst man in wealth and store,
Though foolishly he lost the same,
Decaying more and more,
Till he became
Most poore:
With thee
O let me rise
As larks, harmoniously,
And sing this day thy victories:
Then shall the fall further the flight in me.

Easter

¶ Easter wings.

My tender age in sorrow did beginne:
And still with sicknesses and shame
Thou didst so punish sinne,
That I became
Most thinne.
With thee
Let me combine,
And feel this day thy victorie:
For, if I imp my wing on thine,
Affliction shall advance the flight in me.

H. Ba.

Cambridge poets.

(a) Title-page and an opening of Herbert; *The Temple*, 1633. Herbert was a Cambridge don and University Orator before going to the country parish where he wrote the poems collected in *The Temple*, published in the year of his early death. The book was popular, and went into six editions by 1641.

JUSTA
EDOVARDO KING
naufrago,
ab
Amicis mœrentibus,
amoris
&
μνείας χάριν.

Si rectè calculum ponas, ubique naufragium est.
Pet. Arb.

CANTABRIGIÆ:
Apud *Thomam Buck,* & *Rogerum Daniel,* celeberrimæ
Academiæ typographos. **1638.**

Obsequies to
the memorie
of
Mr EDWARD
KING,

Anno Dom.
1 6 3 8.

Printed by *Th. Buck*, and *R. Daniel*,
printers to the *Universitie* of
Cambridge. 1638.

(b) *Obsequies for Edward King*, 1638. Edward King was a young scholar of great piety and promise, who was drowned when the ship taking him to Ireland was wrecked. A Fellow of Christ's, he was a friend of Milton, who was inspired to write *Lycidas* in his memory. It appeared in this volume of poems published to commemorate King's loss.

21

For we were nurst upon the self-same hill,
Fed the same flock, by fountain, shade, and rill;
Together both, ere the high lawns appear'd
Under the glimmering eye-lids of the morn,
We drove a-field, and both together heard
What time the gray-fly winds her sultry horn,
Batt'ning our flocks with the fresh dews of night,
Oft till the ev'n-starre bright
Toward heav'ns descent had slop'd his burnisht wheel.
Mean while the rurall ditties were not mute,
Temper'd to th' oaten flute;
Rough Satyres danc'd, and Fauns with cloven heel
From the glad sound would not be absent long,
And old Dametas lov'd to heare

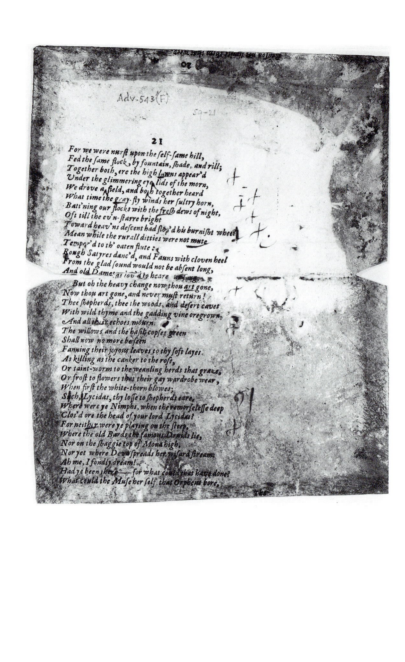

But oh the heavy change now thou art gone,
Now thou art gone, and never must return!
Thee shepherds, thee the woods, and desert caves
With wild thyme and the gadding vine oregrown,
And all their echoes mourn.
The willows and the hasle copses green
Shall now no more be seen
Fanning their joyous leaves to thy soft layes.
As killing as the canker to the rose,
Or taint-worm to the weanling herds that graze,
Or frost to flowers that their gay wardrobe wear,
When first the white-thorn blowes;
Such, Lycidas, thy losse to shepherds eare.
Where were ye Nimphs, when the remorseless deep
Clos'd ore the head of your lord Lycidas?
For neither were ye playing on the steep,
Where the old Bards the famous Druids lie,
Nor on the shaggie top of Mona high,
Nor yet where Deva spreads her wisard stream:
Ah me, I fondly dream!
Had ye been there— for what could that have done?
What could the Muse her self, that Orpheus bore,

Sunk though he be beneath the watry floore:
So sinks the day-starre in the Ocean bed,
And yet anon repairs his drooping head,
And tricks his beams, and with new spangled ore
Flames in the forehead of the morning skie:
So Lycidas sunk low, but mounted high
Through the dear might of him that walk'd the waves;
Where other groves, and other streams along,
With Nectar pure his oazie locks he laves,
And heares the unexpressive nuptiall song;
There entertain him all the Saints above
In solemn troups and sweet societies,
That sing, and singing in their glory move,
And wipe the tears for ever from his eyes.
Now, Lycidas, the shepherds weep no more;
Henceforth thou art the Genius of the shore
In thy large recompense, and shalt be good
To all that wander in that perilous flood.

    Thus sang the uncouth swain to th' oaks and rills,
While the still morn went out with sandals gray;
He touch'd the tender stops of various quills,
With eager thought warbling his Dorick lay:
And now the sunne had stretch'd out all the hills,
And now was dropt into the western bay;
At last he rose, and twitch'd his mantle blew,
To morrow to fresh woods and pastures new.

[handwritten annotation in right margin:] oozie
in the blest kingdoms
meeke of joy and Lov

J. Milton.

(c) *Lycidas*; proof-sheet and printed version. The copy in the University
Library is corrected in a hand thought to be that of Milton himself.

time he would also print a genuinely learned book for a Cambridge author. But to cover his overheads he would need to print standard selling-items, the bread-and-butter titles which reprint every year or two and always sell out. More and more, as the century progressed, he found himself doing this as a subcontractor for a larger printer–bookseller in London. To us now, all this seems very small beer, but the evolution of an important institution starts from such small beginnings. It was dissatisfaction with the existing state of affairs that led to the next evolutionary stage, Bentley's revival of the Press.

BENTLEY'S PUBLIC PRESS

In June 1696 the Chancellor of the University, the Duke of Somerset, sent a letter to the Senate outlining what he modestly called a 'short and imperfect scheme of some thoughts of mine'. The thoughts were actually those of Richard Bentley, who with some other senior Cambridge men probably calculated that to get the Chancellor to propose the scheme was the best way to have it sympathetically considered, especially since Somerset was rich as well as powerful, could and did offer to back the idea with his own funds, and could persuade others to do so as well.

The scheme itself was 'to have a Press once more erected at Cambridge' – which shows how far the University was from being satisfied with present arrangements. The major incentive was that such a press would recover 'the fame of your own printing those great and excellent writings that are so frequently published from the members of your own body; which though very learned sometimes have been much prejudiced by the unskilful hands of uncorrect printers'.

At this time Bentley was only thirty-four, but had already become famous as a classical scholar and intellectual. He was quick to see, for instance, the significance of Newton's work, and in his Boyle lectures of 1692 had made this public. He was a friend of Newton, Locke, Wren and Evelyn, was a Fellow of the Royal Society, and was in due course to become Master of Trinity and a formidable controversialist. It was Bentley who was given virtual plenipotentiary power by Grace of the Senate to set up the new-style press. He had in mind a good printer and manager, Cornelius Groeneveldt, known as Crownfield, and Crownfield went off to his native Holland to buy types and equipment and bring them back.

An agreement was reached with the old-style Press, managed by the ageing Hayes. The Stationers, being told that what was proposed was a learned press, which would not compete with their much more commercially oriented business, made no objection, and simply went on with what they were doing. So the two businesses operated side by side – literally, since Crownfield set up his press in a little converted medical theatre in Queens' Lane, next door to the larger printing house which Hayes continued to run for a

The Queens' Lane site. This pen-and-ink drawing from the nineteenth century looks down Queens' Lane. The low building on the right-hand side is the little theatre in which Bentley's press was first established: you can still see the door with the classical pediment in the wall of St Catharine's Fellows' Carpark. Just outside the picture to the right is John Hayes's larger printing house, where the garden of the Master's Lodge now stands.

few more years. The Stationers finally left Cambridge when Hayes died in 1705, but continued to pay the University an annual sum, provided that the new Press would not compete with it for its best-selling titles; so there was an aftermath of the old bad system. In the middle of 1707, Crownfield moved his men and equipment into the bigger building which Hayes had run and where printing was carried on for the rest of the century.

The truly important aspects of Bentley's revival are that he took the Press much more under the operational control of the University itself. Instead of just licensing a tradesman, so that he was so to speak 'by appointment' Printer to the University but operated very largely on his own account, the University now owned its own presses and types, rented its own accommodation, employed Crownfield, first as 'Inspector', then in 1705 as Printer, and supervised the business. This last aspect was the most important: the University appointed a body of senior scholars, called at first the 'Curators' of the Press – the predecessors of the later Syndics. They met regularly, kept minutes, and Crownfield reported to them. They supervised the accounts and out of their own funds made up any deficit on the year's trading. Ever since Bentley's time the University has exercised this responsibility for its own Press, and has done so through a committee of dons, the Press Syndicate.

At this time the notion of publishing was hardly developed. The first real publisher in England, Jacob Tonson,

PHILOSOPHIÆ
NATURALIS
PRINCIPIA
MATHEMATICA.

AUCTORE
ISAACO NEWTONO,
EQUITE AURATO.

EDITIO SECUNDA AUCTIOR ET EMENDATIOR.

CANTABRIGIÆ, MDCCXIII.

Newton's *Principia*.

(a) The first edition of Newton's *Principia* had appeared in London in 1687, and went quickly out of print. Meanwhile Newton's own thought had progressed. Bentley acted as publisher, even as designer; but a young Cambridge mathematician, Roger Cotes, acted as mathematical adviser and editor. Printing took from 1709 until 1713. The Cambridge emblem on the title-page, with angel supporters, was engraved by Simon Gribelin.

SECTIO IV.

*De Inventione Orbium Ellipticorum, Parabolicorum & Hyperbolico-
rum ex umbilico dato.*

LEMMA XV.

Si ab Ellipseos vel Hyperbolæ cujusvis umbilicis duobus S, H, *ad
punctum quodvis tertium* V *inflectantur rectæ duæ* SV, HV,
quarum una HV *æqualis sit axi principali figuræ, altera* SV *a
perpendiculo* TR *in se demisso bi-*
secetur in T; *perpendiculum illud*
TR *sectionem Conicam alicubi tan-*
get: & contra, si tangit, erit HV
æqualis axi principali figuræ.

Secet enim perpendiculum *TR* re-
ctam *HV* productam, si opus fuerit,
in *R₃* & jungatur *SR*. Ob æquales
TS, TV, æquales erunt & rectæ *SR, VR* & anguli *TRS, TRV.*
Unde punctum *R* erit ad Sectionem Conicam, & perpendiculum
TR tanget eandem: & contra. *Q. E. D.*

PROPOSITIO XVIII. PROBLEMA X.

*Datis umbilico & axibus principalibus describere Trajectorias Ellipti-
cas & Hyperbolicas, quæ transsibunt per puncta data, & rectas po-
sitione datas contingent.*

Sit *S* communis umbilicus figurarum; *AB* longitudo axis prin-
cipalis Trajectoriæ cujusvis; *P* punctum per quod Trajectoria debet transire; & *TR* recta quam debet tangere. Centro *P* intervallo *AB − SP,* si orbita sit Ellipsis, vel *AB + SP,* si ea sit Hy-
perbola, describatur circulus *HG.* Ad tangentem *TR* demittatur
perpendiculum *ST,* & producatur idem ad *V,* ut sit *TV* æqualis
ST; centroque *V* & intervallo *AB* describatur circulus *FH.* Hac
I 2   methodo

THE
WORKS OF THAT

FAMOVS AND WORTHIE

Minister of Christ, in the Universitie of CAM-
BRIDGE, M. W. PERKINS :

Gathered into one volume, and newly corrected
according to his owne copies.

WITH DISTINCT CHAPTERS, AND CONTENTS
of euery booke, and a generall Table of the whole.

Isa. 57. 1.
*The righteous perisheth, and no man considereth it in heart: mercifull men are taken away,
and no man vnderstandeth that the righteous is taken away from the euill to come.*
2. Pet. 1. 15.
*Neuerthelesse I will endeauour alwaies . that ye also may be able to haue remembrance of
these things after my departing.*

LVCEM·E·MET·POCVLA·SACRA·HINC

ALMA
MATER
CANTA
BRIGIA

Printed by IOHN LEGAT, Printer to the
Vniuersitie of CAMBRIDGE. 1603.

The Cambridge Emblem.

(a) In Perkins, *Works*, 1603. The puritan preacher and writer William
Perkins was a best-selling author in the early seventeenth century; his works
were influential in the American colonies, being carried there by early

immigrants with a Cambridge education. The Cambridge emblem first used
here is an allegorical figure of 'kind mother Cambridge' whose breasts flow
with the milk of sound learning and piety; one hand holds the sun of
revealed truth, the other a cup into which the blessings of Heaven neatly
pour. On either side green bay trees flourish. The wording has become the
University's accepted motto: 'From hence issue light and the sacred cup.'
(b) In Bentley's Horace, 1711. By Bentley's time the image had been made
less rustic; our Mother has some clothing and a more elegant posture. The
river-god in the foreground, looking across to the Wren Library, Great St
Mary's and King's, is almost certainly Milton's 'Camus [the Cam], reverend
sire,...footing slow, His mantle hairy and his bonnet sedge...' in *Lycidas*.

had embarked on his career and turned to the Cambridge Press to produce some of the handsome editions of the classical authors, which he sold to gentlemen for their libraries, and the cheaper editions, which he sold in larger numbers to students. But not many people yet distinguished the entrepreneurial character of the publisher from the productive role of the printer and the selling role of the bookseller. Bentley himself did. He was his own publisher and most skilfully organised the most important product of the new Press – the second edition, in 1713, of Newton's *Principia*. This is one of the most important scientific works ever printed and the new edition was revised substantially by Newton himself, with whom Bentley had by now a rather complicated relationship. Bentley made a substantial profit from the venture; meanwhile his handsome Cambridge edition of Horace (1711) secured his reputation as a scholar.

One difficulty with any enterprise which depends on the energy and skill of one or two men is that the men get old or tired or interested in other things, and the enterprise loses its impetus. In the end it may be run by people who were not there when it was started and do not share the missionary zeal of the pioneers. By the 1730s Crownfield was old and Bentley was embattled and eccentric. The first use of the word 'Syndicate' in connection with the Press occurs in 1733; in that year and in 1737 Syndicates were set up to enquire into the running of the Press. They found that the annual loss was rising and, if it had been taken into proper account over the years, it was so large as to make it questionable whether the business was well run. The supervision of the Syndicate itself seemed sporadic. But already the Press was quite a large enterprise by the standards of the time; Crownfield had four printing-presses, employed seven compositors and had other staff. All the evidence suggests that the Press needed access to the London market, and needed to engage in forms of trading which would pay the overheads and bring in a regular surplus if it was also to be able to engage in its primary objective of scholarly publishing. That is in fact the lesson which had been clear to close observers from the beginning: it is so to speak Lesson One in university press publishing. But it was lost sight of from time to time and had to be painfully relearned. In the 1730s, as Bentley's Press lost impetus, the Syndicate pointed out that the failure to engage in the Bible trade was a failure to exercise a valuable right.

THE EIGHTEENTH CENTURY

By this time the Stationers were no longer a serious trading entity, but individual members still regarded the university presses as rivals to be smothered if possible, and taken over if not. In particular the Barker dynasty had been succeeded by the Basketts, and John Baskett, the King's Printer, at one time also held the office of Printer at Oxford and had a share in the King's Scottish Printer's Patent, so he was a monopolist on a grand scale. But opinion was never in favour of monopolies, which seemed a way of holding the public to ransom, and as the eighteenth century went on and theories of free trade acquired intellectual force, the old system seemed less and less defensible. It had always been important that the university presses should seem like the desirable exceptions to a monopoly, rather than members of a ring. This argument was additional to the ones brought forward by a Syndicate of 1741 in advising the Press

to undertake the printing of a Bible of such a size as is of most general demand, and this they did, 1. in order to serve the public with a more beautiful and correct edition than can be easily found, 2. for the honour of the University, which would be advanced by such a work being well executed at their Press, 3. that by being secure of constant employment for them, they may be always able to retain a number of good hands ready for any work that shall be brought in, 4. because they believe a considerable profit may accrue to the University by printing Bibles.

The then Printer, Joseph Bentham, began to print Bibles

and Prayer Books, at first rather cautiously. He was supported by a London agent, Charles Bathurst of Fleet Street, who is named on the title pages. With a London outlet secured, the Press could build a certain volume of trade on the Bible and the Anglican Book of Common Prayer, which since the Act of Uniformity of 1662 had been prescribed by law as the service book of the Church of England, and was therefore as much a 'standard selling line' as the so-called Authorised Version of the Bible. Cambridge made good the Syndicate's points 1 and 2 by commissioning two textual editors, Dr Parris and Dr Therond, to prepare a careful revision of the text, which had by now been considerably corrupted by over a century of mostly careless printing. This was the 'Cambridge standard' edition of 1762, which was used subsequently as a setting-text for other printings.

Bentham's Bibles and Prayer Books are handsome enough and still make desirable antiquarian purchases; but real beauty in Bible-printing was provided by John Baskerville's folio Bible of 1763. Baskerville, originally a writing-master, and interested in letter-forms and typographical style, had become a rich man in trade, and was able to indulge his passion for producing beautiful printed books. He managed to get himself appointed as Cambridge Printer, alongside Bentham, and so acquired the right to print a Bible. It uses his own type-design and printed ornaments, his special ink, and his method of hot-pressing the printed sheets to produce a brilliant black on white. It is undoubtedly one of the dozen

THE

CONTAINING THE

OLD TESTAMENT

AND

THE NEW:

Tranflated out of the

AND

With the former TRANSLATIONS

Diligently Compared and Revifed,

By His MAJESTY's Special Command.

APPOINTED TO BE READ IN CHURCHES.

CAMBRIDGE,

Printed by *JOHN BASKERVILLE,* Printer to the UNIVERSITY.

M DCC LXIII.

CUM PRIVILEGIO.

Baskerville's Bible. Baskerville was a great designer, but not so successful as publisher. 1250 copies of the Bible were printed, but it sold slowly, and was eventually remaindered.

truly great printed Bibles and provided a standard and an example when Cambridge produced a revival of design in printing in the twentieth century.

Baskett cannot have been pleased to see Cambridge re-enter the Bible business, but did not attack on this front. He sued the Press in 1741 for printing an abridgement of an Act of Parliament which infringed his other monopoly. After a series of actions in the courts, the University was vindicated in 1755; the Court of King's Bench decided that 'by virtue of the Letters Patent ... the Chancellor Masters and Scholars of the University are INTRUSTED, with a concurrent authority, to print Acts of Parliament and abridgements...' – these being among the 'all kinds of books' which would also include Bibles and Prayer Books. One of the judges who made the decision sent a copy of it in a letter to the great jurist Blackstone, who was at that moment reorganising the Oxford Press, adding:

The words underlined were thrown in, by way of an intimation to the University, that we consider the powers given by the Letters Patent as a trust reposed in that learned body, for public benefit, for the advancement of literature, and not to be transferred upon lucrative views to other hands. I hope both the universities will always consider the royal grants in that light.

This was a most important statement. It is another instance of the constitutional importance of the charter, but also a significant reinterpretation, since the word 'trust' brings in a whole set of ethical constraints which had not been clearly identified until this time. It was being said that the University could not from now on farm out its right to others for purely commercial exploitation, nor could it treat that right as purely commercial itself. 'Public benefit' and 'the advancement of literature' (in the old wide sense of any serious reading-matter) had now to be the criterion of the whole enterprise.

This role of the University Presses was also recognised by the Almanac Duty Act of 1781. This was the last stage of a dispute which began in the 1770s when a quarrelsome bookseller infringed the Stationers' Company's right to print almanacs. Now almanacs were probably the most profitable kind of printing there was; almost every literate person bought one every year. They were a kind of calendar and reference work, with astrological as well as astronomical information, and could be little books or broadsheets hung on the wall. During the previous century Cambridge had printed them in large numbers, often for the Company, but had in 1777 renewed a covenant of forbearance with the Company by which for an annual payment of £500 it agreed not to exercise its right to print them. So the University was to that extent damaged if the Stationers' monopoly was thrown open. However, the public mood was against the monopoly, so that in 1781 the two University Presses were granted an annual payment of £500 from the receipts of the duty which the government now imposed on almanacs. The ground of this award was that in the past

the money so received by them has been laid out and expended in promoting different branches of literature and science, to the great increase of religion and learning, and the general benefit and advantage of these realms.

The sum payable under the Act – and at first it had very considerable purchasing power – was by Grace of 1782 placed at the disposal of the Press Syndicate for the publication of new works or new editions of old works. Almanac duty was abolished early in the next century, but for two hundred years, until its abolition in 1985, the Press received, and carefully allocated to specific works of learning, this subvention from public funds – the only such money it ever received. By 1985 the value of the benefit had become negligible in economic terms, but the Press was sorry to lose this public testimony to its contribution to the objectives set out in the original Act.

So, at the end of its second century, the Press had evolved in important ways. It was beginning to be recognised, both within the Press and outside, that it had a disinterested public function, which was to advance knowledge by its publications. It was recognised also that if it had a part in the privilege of printing Bibles and Prayer Books, this was not simply in order to have two best-sellers permanently on its list; it was *exempt* from a monopoly, not the holder of a monopoly, and it had to use the product of this advantage in order to carry out its primary function. This had been recognised by the State, which actually made a contribution out of tax-payers' money in the shape of the almanac payment. It had evolved from being simply the little printing house of an otherwise independent printer – there was now a permanent set of premises. And, importantly, the whole operation was now owned, supervised and controlled by the University through its system of committees or Syndicates, which became more and more systematic and business-like as time went by. By the end of the century, the Press's business was capable of growing substantially, being firmly founded on the printing of the Bible and the Prayer Book. What was needed to bring this about was the technology introduced in the next generation or two. For meanwhile, if Gutenberg had come back to life, he would have seen a hand-printing process still very much like that which he had invented: single types laboriously set by hand, and printed on a wooden press capable of perhaps 1,000 impressions of one sheet in a good day, and the books bound by hand in single copies. Above all, any printer who entered the Bible trade found that he was setting by hand one of the longest books of all. Labour was cheaper than type-metal and very few printers had enough type to set the whole text of the Bible: they had to print a sheet or two, disperse the type, set the next sheet, and so on. Because it was always being reset, often in a hurry, the text was always in danger of being degraded by misprints. What was needed was a technical device for holding a text available for constant reprinting without constant resetting.

THE EARLY NINETEENTH CENTURY

And this was one of the first technological innovations of the nineteenth century; moreover it was pioneered at Cambridge. The inventor Lord Stanhope perfected a device for making stereotype plates, by making a mould of the whole surface of a page of type and then casting plates from the mould. The technique was communicated first to Cambridge and rapidly applied to Bibles. By an extraordinary coincidence the British and Foreign Bible Society, set up in 1804 as a missionary endeavour to supply Bibles cheap, or if necessary free, to the growing population of urban Britain, then to Europe and then to the Third World, needed a supply of mass-produced Bibles and turned first of all to Cambridge, which in 1805 produced the Cambridge Stereotype Bible specially for this market. Supplying the BFBS and other missionary societies with very large numbers of Bibles became the foundation of Cambridge's fortunes in the nineteenth century, so that it became a printing business of significant size, and a substantial employer of skilled labour.

The old printing house, built in 1655, was now at the end of its useful life. The Press began by crossing the street, as it were; it built a warehouse in Silver Street in 1786, and a stereotype foundry next to it after 1804. It had begun to occupy the island site between Silver Street and Mill Lane and in the end it filled the whole area between Trumpington Street and Laundress Lane. The most striking of these

The Stanhope Press. For nearly four hundred years, printing presses had been made of wood. The iron press permitted much greater accuracy of register, and a greater pressure over a larger printing area, as well as stability and an indefinitely long life.

THE

NEW

TESTAMENT

OF

OUR LORD AND SAVIOUR

JESUS CHRIST:

———

TRANSLATED OUT OF THE ORIGINAL GREEK;

AND WITH

THE FORMER TRANSLATIONS DILIGENTLY COMPARED AND REVISED,

BY HIS MAJESTY'S SPECIAL COMMAND.

———

Appointed to be read in Churches.

CAMBRIDGE STEREOTYPE EDITION.

CAMBRIDGE:

STEREOTYPED AND PRINTED BY R. WATTS,

FOR THE UNIVERSITY;

And Sold by Messrs. *Rivington*, St. Paul's Church-Yard; Mr. *Mawman*, in the
Poultry, London; and Mr. *Deighton*, Cambridge.

July, 1805.

The Cambridge Stereotype Bible, 1805. At last successive printings were
possible from one setting, which could be corrected in detail, and so permit
gradual improvement rather than progressive degradation of the text. The
edition was prepared for the newly founded British and Foreign Bible
Society of London, a charitable enterprise which attracted great public
support and soon found itself supplying Europe (see George Borrow's *Bible
in Spain*) and the newly colonised territories of the Third World.

buildings is the one it still occupies – the Pitt Building, with its pinnacled façade, tower and oriel window facing Pembroke College, where William Pitt the Younger, the great prime minister and war-leader, had been an undergraduate. He had died in 1806, a scheme to put up a statue in London had been over-subscribed and it was thought highly appropriate to take the residue, add to it, buy a site and put up a building opposite his college for the permanent occupation of the University Press. It was designed by Edward Blore, the architect of Sir Walter Scott's house at Abbotsford. It was completed and ceremonially opened in 1833. It is not, as you can see by looking at it, a very practical building for use as a factory or even an office, but it has real style and presence, and presents a dignified and attractive face to the world. Behind it, from the 1830s onwards, successive Printers put up the plainer but still handsome buildings which form the court and the complex set of intercommunicating premises all the way to Laundress Lane. The Printer had a house on the Mill Lane side.

While this was going on, printing was being mechanised. The first iron presses were also invented by Stanhope; more important, the first steam-driven reciprocating presses were perfected by König and Bauer, and began to operate in London in 1814, printing *The Times* newspaper. The manufacture of paper was also mechanised and paper became cheap. By the 1840s the Press was using steam-driven machines to print Bibles, against some initial opposition

The Pitt Building.

The Pitt Press.

CAMBRIDGE University ALMANACK, 1834.

from conservative buyers. But books went on being hand-set throughout the century.

By the 1850s the Press was a printing house of substantial size. More money had been spent on its buildings and equipment – from its own funds and the public subscription for the Pitt Building – than on any other University department and it was probably the biggest employer of labour in Cambridge except for the University itself. But as at previous times in its history it was facing a crisis, partly because of its constitutional arrangements – the way it was run, and its relationship with the University – partly because those arrangements did not provide effective business leadership. At the beginning of the century the Printer was, as he always had been, an ordinary master-printer who happened to be working for the University, though he was still able to take on work for other publishers. And there, really, was the rub. The Press was not in any important

Cambridge Almanac for 1834, showing the Pitt Building. '... That Press from which emanate works of enlightened Literature and profound Science' in the words of Lord Camden, Chancellor of the University, calling for funds. The finished building has this hopeful and confident air, though it was not, for a hundred years, used extensively by the Press itself. It housed the Registrary until the building of the University Library enabled him to move out to the Old Schools site in the 1930s. In 1963 the Syndicate began to hold its meetings in the great vaulted gothic room behind the oriel window, and it still meets there on alternate Friday afternoons in term, receiving reports on the businesses from the officers of the Press, and deciding which books and journals shall be published. In the picture, the house just behind on the right has not yet been replaced by the expansion towards the river of the whole Press site which took place in the nineteenth century.

Photographs of the interior of the old Printing House. These photographs may have been taken in the 1940s, but they show a printing house and printing practices very little changed in the previous century.
(a) The compositor is standing at a case ('upper' for capitals, 'lower' for the rest) such as Thomas Thomas would have recognised, setting type by hand in a composing 'stick'.

(b) Another compositor working on type in a 32-page forme, tightening the wooden 'quoins' which hold the type in place.

(c) An apprentice making a stereotype mould by beating a sheet of papier-mâché, laid over the type surface, with a metal brush. This forces the type surface into the papier-mâché, so that an intaglio of the whole page is created, and can be used as a mould from which a replica can be cast as a single plate of type-metal.

(d) The machine room, steam driven from the 1840s, electrically powered in this century, but using basically the same kind of reciprocating machine in which paper sheets are caught by, and swiftly passed round a cylinder, and pressed on to the surface of the formes of type, moving equally swiftly forward to meet the cylinder carrying the paper, and back again for the next pass. Walking down Silver Street, pedestrians would hear the tramp of the machines, like mechanical waves breaking.

degree a publisher; though the Syndicate felt a duty to publish a small stream of works of learning, this really was only a trickle. It justified the whole enterprise without providing a real basis of prosperity, or even importantly supplementing or diversifying the printing business, which was dangerously concentrated on Bibles. The Bible trade remained, for all the strange English institution of privileged printing, quite a cut-throat business, with the Queen's Printer in London and the Oxford Press both dwarfing Cambridge, and the Bible Society, with its charitable aims, driving down prices. Already in the early decades of the century there were official enquiries into the Press's fortunes, and the Printers can be found producing pamphlets saying they did not see, how they could be doing any better. Nor could they, under the system they had to operate. Meanwhile from 1843 to 1863 the brothers Macmillan ran a very successful bookshop on the old corner site at the end of Trinity Street. They talked to their distinguished University customers, and realised that in them they had a constituency of authors who were to be had for the asking. More important, they asked them. They began to build up a publishing business, indeed an empire, under the noses of the Printer to the University and the Press Syndicate. Admittedly, the Press got a good deal of the printing, but for a generation' it failed to learn the real lesson that publishing, even scholarly publishing, is an active, not a passive enterprise, such that when Cambridge did begin to compete, it took nearly a century to catch up in some subjects.

Since the Press was a department of the University, it could not, fortunately, escape the scrutiny of the Royal Commission which in 1852 reported on the whole University and recommended radical reform. Just before the Commission began its enquiry, the Press was enquiring into itself, and its own report suggested that its trade was in decline, and the business was over-capitalised, over-staffed, and under-employed. But nobody within the enterprise could see any other way of using the resources, so there was a move to shed staff and reduce the scale of the whole operation. The Royal Commission, on the other hand, took a characteristically robust Victorian view, and saw matters in very Victorian terms. It was sure the Press could do better, but only on one condition:

It is only by associating printers or publishers in some species of co-partnership with the University, or leasing the Press to them, that any considerable return can hereafter be expected from the capital which has been invested in it... We are satisfied that no Syndicate, however active and well chosen, can replace the intelligent and vigilant superintendence of those whose fortune in life is dependent upon its [the Press's] success.

That is to say, the University now needed to move entirely away from the notion that it could have a 'public press' – a building and equipment – could appoint successive competent persons as Printer, and those printers could for a time move in and exploit the facility with no particular policy or long-term view. They could also do a little publishing and bookselling on their own account, and not mind very much also handling the occasional learned book that the Syndicate chose to publish on *its* own account. That was the eighteenth-century, even the seventeenth-century pattern. What the Commission was now pointing out was that the Press had a substantial capital which needed to be employed in an entrepreneurial way and since the Syndicate itself was not entrepreneurial it had better enter into partnership with someone who would bring into that partnership more capital and above all the ability to employ it properly, indeed to exploit it. Such a person would want a return on his capital, but that is what the University ought to want too, and it could arrange to share the return with the partner. Put like that, it all seems a little crude, and so it was, but it also has a bracing nineteenth-century business-like briskness. It took the University, that is to say the Syndicate, a long time to see that these terms themselves were too simple and too little adapted to the peculiar nature of the University's function; were in fact a false analysis based on textbook economic and accounting notions – a caricature of capitalism. Meanwhile the Press was saved: more because the right man was brought in and did the right things than because he was brought in on the right terms.

THE PARTNERSHIP

On 31 May 1854 a Grace proposed to the Senate a partnership with Mr George Seeley of Fleet St London, Bookseller, and Mr Charles John Clay, MA of Trinity College and of Bread St Hill London, Printer. It was passed. Clay was a member of the well-known dynasty of printers. His father had been an apprentice at the Press after leaving the Perse School, so there was an old Cambridge connection, strengthened by his own membership of Trinity. He had thought of entering the Church and becoming a don, but had gone into the family business in London; the Subsyndicate acting as search committee was guided to him as potential Printer and Partner, and the negotiations were successful. Under the terms of the new agreement Clay and Seeley injected capital into the Press, so that they had a half-share in it. Seeley and Clay were 'to transact the whole business', with Seeley acting as bookseller–agent in London. The partners and the Syndicate were both to have a guaranteed return on capital, and any surplus was to be shared. The agreement was to run for fourteen years.

Having seen the new relationship set up, and having helped to reorganise the Cambridge printing and the London agency, Seeley dropped out of the partnership, leaving Clay with a half-share in the business, and effectively the organising and managing brain of the whole of the Press until his resignation in 1893: an extraordinarily long and very successful term of office.

He began by reorganising the printing business, which was his family expertise, concentrating at first on the Bible and Prayer Book trade, where Cambridge had lost its market share; this had to be built up again as the foundation on which all else rested. The Syndicate itself was reconstructed; members were chosen for specific interests and abilities, and were appointed for a fixed term of office. Though the Vice-Chancellor was *ex officio* Chairman, Vice-Chancellors changed every year, so the practice grew up of having a Vice-Chancellor's Deputy, who acted as Chairman for a period of several years, even many years, thus providing continuity of supervision. There developed a happy relationship between the Chairman and the Printer, especially between Clay and James Cartmell, Master of Christ's, who was the first real Chairman of the Press Syndicate. From this time on, there is a consistent record in the Syndicate Minute Books of decisions taken at regular meetings. These are in the hand of the Chairman, who also conducted a good deal of the correspondence on behalf of the Syndicate, until the volume of business became such that it called for a Secretary, to use the old English term for the Chief Executive who conducts the business of an official body by providing its meetings with papers and verbal advice, and then superintends the sending of letters and memoranda which carry out its deliberations.

During Clay's first decade or so as Printer, while he concentrated on reorganising the printing business itself, since it was by far the largest part of the Press's output, publishing remained a tiny element: a few learned books a year, each of them with a very small slow sale. Things began to change in the 1870s, and the significant aspect of the change is that it showed an active desire to expand the business by commissioning books, and to do this in areas where large sales could be expected over the long term. In particular the national growth of secondary education and the associated system of public examinations, some of which were organised by the University itself, presented a new market for schoolbooks. In 1874 Cambridge published the first volumes in the Pitt Press Series of edited texts. In the end there were 200 volumes in this series, and many of them had a long life and sold hundreds of thousands of copies; they led on to later ventures such as Verity's editions of Shakespeare and Milton, which sold millions.

At the same time Cambridge embarked with Oxford on the publication of the Revised Version of the Bible: the New Testament of 1881 was followed by the whole new Bible in 1885. This produced unprecedented sales and required modern marketing techniques. The Press had prepared the ground by opening its own London Office, first in Paternoster Row in 1873, and then in Ave Maria Lane in 1884: this last move was just in time to handle the Revised Version. At first thought of as a 'Warehouse', mainly stocking Bibles, the London Office soon became a sales department, a headquarters for representatives, an advertising office, and increasingly an accounts department. It was a further recognition of the problem which had faced Cambridge

Printers since 1584, as long as London was the centre of the booktrade, both nationally, and increasingly internationally. For almost exactly 100 years longer, it seemed necessary to be at that centre of the British communications network and publishing world in order to compete successfully for authors and sales in a nation-wide market. And of course, once the machine was set up, it had to be used; work had to be found.

The growth of the business meant that the volume of correspondence and other paperwork was such that it was no longer possible for a part-time Chairman to consider undertaking it. A Secretary had to be appointed; and in 1874 Clay was given the unpaid post, so that he was both Printer and Secretary to the Syndicate, and Manager of the London Warehouse. The Partnership was renewed in 1876 and 1886.

It can be said that Cambridge publishing really took off in the 1880s, and has been accelerating ever since. It may seem strange that in such a long history the modern aspect should be so recent a growth, but that is the nature of the evolutionary process. It can always be said, and always will, that the present state, today's state, is the only true state, and the day before yesterday already looks quaint. But the principle of growth with change is continuous, with sometimes rapid fluctuations. The Partnership with the Clays, which lasted from 1854 until 1916, looks like the longest period of constitutional stability in this history. It leads into the modern era, and yet the idea of a partnership with a professional printer, who would come into the business and run it in partnership with the University, is strikingly continuous with the arrangements of 1584 or any period afterward. On the other hand, the idea that this partnership was for profit, and that the printer-partner would take his profit out of the business, was strikingly in conflict with the idea which far-sighted people had had in the seventeenth and eighteenth centuries of the Press as trust or as charitable trader, where a trading surplus went back into the system in order to fund it, and no outsider-shareholder could benefit personally. This, precisely, was what was wrong with the otherwise excellent arrangement with the Clays. It began to be perceived in the University; and when the Partnership was successively renewed, the University constantly increased its share, working towards total ownership.

But the first step towards that control had to be the parallel evolution of a management-structure which combined the business competence of a Clay with an internal loyalty to the ultimate purposes of the Press considered as a scholarly printing and publishing enterprise. R. T. Wright, Fellow of Christ's, joined the Syndicate in 1887 and became very active and specifically interested in increasing the volume of publishing. In 1891, he was appointed Secretary to the Syndicate, and took up the office on 1 January 1892. So, for a year, the Press which had sometimes had three printers had two secretaries. In 1893 Clay retired, though his two sons remained partners.

Wright's priorities were clear. The printing house was well run, large and prosperous. He inherited a small publishing list; when it had been displayed in its first catalogue, in 1875, it occupied sixteen pages and could also be printed at the end of books without difficulty. It was possible for the Clays and their staff to think of the Syndicate's publishing as a sort of high-minded hobby; or a small trickle of work for them to do; or a way of losing a little money each year. If the trickle became a large stream it threatened to lose a lot of money, which the printing business would have to generate; it would also diminish the Partners' profits. It was Wright's task to build up Cambridge publishing and to see that it did more than break even, so he had to use skill to get the Syndicate to commission and to accept books. By 1900 he could point to a modest surplus on publishing. Since 1894 he had had his own office: the little red-brick building on the Mill Lane side of the Old Press Site currently occupied by the Law Faculty. It had a large room where the Syndicate met until 1963, with the growing library of their publications round the walls marking the results of their deliberations, and with one or two adjoining offices for the Secretary's tiny staff.

THE PARTNERSHIP ENDS

In 1905, when the Partnership was renewed, the publishing business was taken entirely into the control of the Syndicate, and the Clays' share in the printing business was reduced to one tenth. C. F. Clay was appointed salaried manager of the London Office, which had just moved to Fetter Lane. When John Clay, the Printer, died in 1916, the Partnership was finally dissolved. The new Printer, J. B. Peace, an engineer, had been a Syndic; so for the first time the heads of both parts of the Press were appointed by and were entirely responsible to the Press Syndicate, which was now at last fully in control of the whole operation of a substantial printing and publishing business. No outsider had managerial status; still less did any outside share-holder have entitlement to any share of the profit – a word which can only be used of an enterprise undertaken in the Victorian spirit of the Royal Commissioners of 1854: the whole-hearted pursuit of a return on capital.

Wright retired in 1911, having set Cambridge publishing firmly on the road. He had the advantage of working at the time when the University had entered on its own golden age. After the Royal Commission, new subjects were founded and attracted scholars of world-wide renown. Above all, the foundation of the Cavendish Laboratory led to the great succession of Cambridge physicists, from Clerk Maxwell and Kelvin and Thomson to Rutherford. The Press published them all. It is to Wright that we owe the establishment of the Press as a scientific and mathematical publisher, as a publisher of journals, of the great collaborative histories initiated by the Cambridge Modern History, planned in 1896 and published in 1902, and, importantly, of the notion of the series of monographs which make available the best research in certain subjects. In fact series publishing is one of the Cambridge strengths; it had been inaugurated by Clay with the Pitt Press Series and the Cambridge Bible for Schools, and only needed to be transferred to the higher levels of study.

Wright was succeeded by A. R. Waller, who had joined the Press as its first Assistant Secretary to the Syndicate in 1902. Waller developed the publishing element still further, himself edited the Cambridge History of English Literature, and founded the New Shakespeare, edited by John Dover Wilson. But the first world war hindered expansion by disrupting markets and causing costs to escalate. Wright, faced with the small size and the annual fluctuation of the surplus on publishing, wanting to be able to finance an expansion but, knowing that the Press had as a matter of principle to publish books which made a loss or a negligible surplus, realised that the only way to secure the operation was to have an endowment, such as the Colleges did. An endowment could only be built up slowly over the long term from the proceeds of the organic growth of the business itself.

When the war came, all such calculations were blown away. However, there was undoubted growth. By 1900, the Cambridge catalogue listed 500 books; in 1921 there were 2,500 (now, there are over 10,000). There were two ways of looking at this; the heartening way was to count the books which were long-lived because they went on selling and reprinting; the disheartening way was to count the books where a very small first impression was still in print after many years. In fact the Cambridge list began to contain a substantial number of school and university textbooks which went on selling for what by modern standards was an extraordinary number of years. The backlist came to produce some seventy-five per cent of turnover, and could at least finance the output of about one hundred new books annually.

BETWEEN THE WARS

Indeed, between the two wars, the Press settled into a steady state, marked by the partnership of S. C. Roberts as Secretary and Walter Lewis as Printer. Roberts became Secretary in 1922, and had almost at once to find a successor for Peace in 1923. Lewis retired in 1945, Roberts in 1948, so they saw the Press through the inter-war and war years. Roberts's most important innovation was the foundation in 1930 of an agency for Cambridge books and Bibles in the USA, using the Macmillan Company. In 1931 the Cambridge Agency became a distinct unit within the host company and was headed by a young Englishman, a Cambridge graduate, Ronald Mansbridge. It would be hard to exaggerate the importance of this move.

In 1921 the number of people employed in Fetter Lane was 110 and the number at the Printing House was 280. The tiny office of the Secretary was staffed by a mere half-dozen. The relative numbers reflect the balance of trading interests; printing was still the main activity and the main source of

(a)

(b)

A Monotype keyboard (a) and caster (b).

revenue. The Bible was still the mainstay of both printing and publishing, but had by now embarked on a long slow decline, visible in the UK, but offset and concealed for a time by buoyant sales overseas, especially in the USA (indeed the history of the Press was replicated in the USA, where for a long time the Bible 'floated' the whole operation). And for a long time too in the UK, the main calls by representatives were still on the Bible accounts. There were already specialist school representatives, but the books were carried by men who were most interested in selling Bibles. Export sales were beginning to grow, and it was here that it began to be clear that works of science, of learning generally, were genuinely international in their sale if only they were good enough, and that British publishers had an inbuilt advantage in that English was the international language of learning as well as of business. The future – our present – was beginning to declare itself: for instance the possibility that in the 1990s the Press would make several millions of pounds a year in publishing material for the teaching of English as a foreign language. Before the second war, the Press exported about thirty-eight per cent of its product; to us that looks small but at the time it was remarkable.

None the less, it was still the printing which carried the business along at this period. The Printing House could handle much more than the publishing business could produce, and became a supplier to other English publishers. Indeed it became one of the leading English printers, not so much in terms of quantity as in terms of skill and standards, especially its accuracy.

It will be remembered that books went on being hand-set throughout the nineteenth century. It was not until 1913 that the Monotype system of hot-metal mechanised type-setting was introduced at the Press, and at first the new technology had no effect on standards of design. In fact it was felt generally that the appearance of Cambridge books did not match their quality.

It was this that Lewis changed. He came to Cambridge with a reputation for skill in design, and brought with him important friendships, notably with Stanley Morison. Morison was typographical adviser to the Monotype Corporation and to *The Times* as well as to the Press, and he was supervising the introduction of new type-faces, some of them revivals of old styles from the sixteenth century onwards and some of them new designs. The new faces had to be seen in use to be appreciated and at Cambridge many of them were first used in book-design. It was not at all a matter of producing 'fine' printing of the sort that is looked at but never read; it was a matter of using, in complex scholarly books, a suitable type which was skilfully deployed to handle all the features of their structure. Readability, and the users' capacity to find their way round a book that lent itself to being seriously read and constantly used, were more important than the reaction 'how nice it looks'. Though in fact the books did look well, that was a consequence of the intelligence of the design, not an intended effect. It was above all a matter of taking the latest technology, the Monotype keyboard and caster, and fully exploiting its resources in the interests of scholarly printing and publishing. The Press's reputation was highest in the printing of very advanced mathematics, where the layout and spacing of complex formulae makes a crucial difference to lucidity and comprehension. The Press as publisher brought forward works by the leading scientists and mathematicians of the day, and the Printing House gave them classic form.

AFTER 1945

The slow growth of the Press in the 1930s was interrupted by the second world war which, like the previous one, swept aside any plans for long-term financial stability and totally disrupted international trade. Bentley House, the purpose-designed London Office in the Euston Road opened in 1938, had providentially been built well away from the traditional publishers' warehousing area, still centred round St Paul's, which was destroyed by bombing – and with it many publishers' stocks. Even so, chronic paper shortage made it hard to print or to reprint, though the national hunger for something to read meant that everything sold out as soon as it was published. So the Press ended the war with depleted stocks, a backlog of accepted books waiting to be printed, and trading links needing to be re-opened. It was ten years before anything like normality returned. Meanwhile, a half-hearted bid to have the Press exempted from profits-tax, on the ground that its trading was for charitable purposes, was refused by the authorities; and it was felt unpatriotic, in wartime, to appeal.

Lewis was succeeded by Brooke Crutchley as Printer in 1945 and Roberts by R. J. L. Kingsford in 1948. Kingsford's most important achievement was the establishment of a United States Branch in 1948, turning the agency with Macmillan into a fully fledged Cambridge Press office in New York. The growth of sales in the USA was the key to subsequent success worldwide, since what began almost exclusively as a marketing activity naturally suggested the thought that books by US authors would help not only US sales but all sales. Editorial policy itself was affected; it had for a long time been clear that an important book in the English language had a sale outside the English-speaking countries. At the highest intellectual level there is one market: the world. For some books it may not be a large market, so it makes even less sense to split it. Before the war a third or more of sales were export sales; now the proportion began to rise significantly, reaching fifty per cent in 1951 and sixty per cent in 1962. Easily the largest and by far the most prosperous and fastest-moving market was the USA itself. Traditionally, English publishers, with their own access to the old Empire markets, had been content to lease US rights in their books to US publishers. It made better sense to handle this market directly, if one could. The Agency, under

(a)

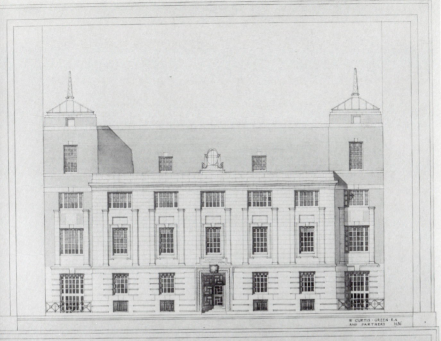

CAMBRIDGE UNIVERSITY PRESS EUSTON ROAD

(b)

The London offices: in Fetter Lane, and Bentley House in the Euston Road.
(a) London, as capital city and centre of the national and international
communications network, was the centre also of the national and the export
booktrade; for centuries, and until very recently, publishers felt it was
essential to have a London outlet. During the seventeenth and early
eighteenth centuries some of the Cambridge printers had London con-
nections of their own, or worked in collaboration with London booksellers
who acted as agents or publishers. In the eighteenth century Cambridge had
its own agent, a bookseller or publisher who regularly handled all
Cambridge Bibles and books. In 1873 the Press started its own London
office in Paternoster Row, and in 1884 moved to Ave Maria Lane; in 1905
it moved to Fetter Lane, shown in the photograph overleaf.
(b) In 1938 the Press built its own large London office, Bentley House, in
the Euston Road. For many years, this remained the only purpose-built
publishing house in London. The illustration is taken from the architect's
drawing.

Mansbridge, had been a half-way house and now the Branch, still under Mansbridge until 1971, became, as the centre of the largest single market, a principal element of the whole editorial and marketing policy of the Press. The Branch began to have its own editors in the mid-1960s, and a small trickle of books by US authors began to grow into a significant stream: over 300 publications a year are now generated by the New York editors.

This was the boom-time. Kingsford retired in 1963, to be succeeded by R. W. David. It was for a few years the happiest and most prosperous time in academic publishing ever. All over the world money was being pumped into higher education; new universities, and especially new university libraries, were being founded and given funds to buy books. At this time growth was measured in the rapidly increasing size of editions and the speed and size of reprints rather than the number of new books published. Even so Cambridge's output of new books doubled to some 200 titles a year, and went on rising. One harbinger of the boom was the New English Bible co-published with Oxford (New Testament 1961, complete Bible 1970). The partnership with Oxford repeated the pattern set up with the Revised Version of the 1880s. Millions of copies were sold and – mark of the persistent features of this history – publication saw the final contest with the then Queen's Printers. Fearing that the new version might threaten their ancient privilege, they published a pirated edition of John's Gospel as a challenge. They were duly taken to court by the University Presses, and in 1963 it

The University Printing House, 1963. On the fifteen-acre site in the
Shaftesbury Road, well away from the narrow streets of the crowded
medieval centre of the town, the Press could design a building where the
production processes could all take place on one level in a rational flow, with
ample space, and with soundproofing for the noisier processes. The office
building was on three floors. There was scope for landscaped open space,
sports facilities – and in the long run for expansion, including the uniting of
the whole Press on the one site.

was established that the NEB was an ordinary copyright, not
to be overridden.

An important change was that the University Printing
House was at last able in 1963 to move from the Mill Lane
site, where for years it had suffered from the cramped
conditions; the old buildings were by now totally unsuited

to modern machines and methods, and modern traffic conditions in Silver Street and Mill Lane made it a nightmare to try to get large trucks loaded with paper or machinery in and out. By a providential piece of foresight the Press was able to buy a fifteen-acre site off Shaftesbury Road away from the city centre, and when the printers had moved to their well-planned new building in 1963 it was clear that there was still a lot of room on the site for future developments.

One effect of that departure was that all sorts of functions to do with design, copy-editing and progress control, which had been handled by the Printer's planning staff, now had to be handled by the old Secretary's office, which had quickly to expand and turn itself into a publisher's editorial and production office. It had to start to organise itself and to think and function – rather late in the day, perhaps – like a modern publisher.

Among other things, this meant having a considered editorial policy which suited both the times and the special nature of the Press. This thinking was now done in the Pitt Building, which the Press at last took over and attempted to use fully. In 1963 the Syndicate finally began to meet in the Oriel Room which had been designed for it in 1832. It had to contemplate three related problems: the implementation of the editorial policy, which increasingly depended on initiatives by a professional staff of commissioning editors, who produced correspondingly long agendas; then the measures which deteriorating trade conditions and the

The Oriel Room, in the Pitt Building. Here, on alternate Friday
afternoons in term-time, the Press Syndicate meets.

chronic weakness of the national economy forced on all firms; then, when finally the crisis came, the fundamental structure of the Press and its purposes. For the boom of the 1960s became the chain of recessions of the 1970s and after. In particular, inflation, which had gone along almost unnoticed at about two or three per cent a year in the 1960s, rose to nine per cent in 1971 and was in continuous double figures from 1974 to 1981. This put extraordinary strains on any business, called for new kinds of thinking, and bankrupted those which could not adapt.

Editorial policy was influenced by two direct experiences – those of the USA and of Africa. The US has been mentioned: as the largest single market for books in the English language with the largest university and college network in the world, it was and is a determinant of all editorial thinking and all marketing of books. The end of British colonial rule in West and East Africa left territories where English was the medium of instruction from the secondary level upwards, where the English system of education had been adapted, and where continuing public examinations were still organised from the Local Examinations Syndicate in Cambridge. There was therefore a market for textbooks linguistically and culturally appropriate to it, preferably by local authors. For a decade or so, the Press specially cultivated Africa and published for it, and it was a good experience in that editors learned how to edit: the problems were an intensification of those presented by any market, and it was important to be shaken out of Anglocentrism. Cambridge withdrew for a number of reasons: the exploitation of the local school market by foreigners, however well intentioned, looked like neo-colonialism and was resented; a local educational publishing industry was bound to replace it; and in any case as trading conditions deteriorated it became increasingly difficult to get money out of these territories. These practical or political reasons were additional to a central imperative where the practical joined the intellectual or philosophical: it made no sense to publish on a large scale for a single market, except for a market as large, as culturally dominant, and as naturally related as the USA.

The whole basis of Cambridge publishing was to be the principle that at the highest level the market is world-wide. One might publish a little locally in order to support the main endeavour, but it was exceedingly important not to do what other British publishers were doing: to set up local empires so concerned with local publishing that they had no time for the genuinely international – and therefore more important – books coming from the centre. So for instance the Australian Branch, founded in 1969 and based on a long experience of local marketing, continued to sell the whole range of Cambridge books; and the books by Australian authors, like the ones by US or Nigerian or indeed authors from any part of the globe, came back to Cambridge, with local and other editorial advice, to be assessed by the Press Syndicate at its meetings in the Syndicate Room in the Pitt Building on alternate Friday afternoons in term-time, starting at 2.15 pm. There was and is one agenda; all the books find their place in it and all are scrutinised by the single body. This reflects the fact that there is one editorial policy, which controls the editorial activity in all the territories. Correspondingly, there is one marketing policy serving the editorial one, so that a Cambridge author who is published in one part of the world will also be published in every other.

One natural effect of the African schoolbook experience was that the Press became a leading publisher in African Studies, and at the higher level, that became a world market. But this was the time when area studies were developing in the universities of the world, so it made sense to enter them all, as it made sense to enter other new subjects like linguistics or sociology, and to reinforce the old subjects where there was already a list, but where there was no great strength. From the late 1950s the sciences, a traditional strength, were being specifically developed by a specialist editor. Since the 1920s there had been a schoolbook editor. From the 1960s on it was recognised that a list could only be developed by a staff of editors who were actively commissioning books, and at the tertiary level this could only be done intelligently by someone who had at least a commitment to the subject, and preferably a qualification in it.

CRISIS AND RECOVERY

By the end of the 1960s there was a potentially disastrous situation: publishing was expanding in terms of new titles, but the sales boom was faltering. Staff had increased to meet that boom, but the Press was also wastefully staffed because of duplication between the London and Cambridge offices. Very rapid increases in costs produced price-rises in new books; but it was not understood that the back-list, which still produced seventy-five per cent of turnover, needed to be re-priced as rapidly and as drastically as the front-list. As it turned out, the Press was trying to recover from faltering new-book sales the whole of a rising overhead and the financing of an expanding list. The Press's books characteristically stay in print for far longer than a commercial publisher's – at that time a twenty-year life was common – so to sell at historic prices on the argument that no extra cost had been incurred was simply to ignore the dwindling purchasing power of money. The Press had no funds of its own, and now at last was facing a crisis in which it was essential to have some endowment. It had to turn to the bank for an overdraft simply to finance the year's operation, and it was in the situation where the overdraft rose remorselessly year by year, the trading position got worse rather than better, and the bank and the University could foresee the day when either the University itself would have to bale out the Press or the bank would foreclose and the Press would either have to scale down its operation or cease trading altogether. The Syndicate, responsible to the University for the running of the Press, and the staff, whose livelihoods were at risk, were truly looking into the abyss.

Behind the scenes, there was no agreement about what to

do; indeed the crisis brought into the open the tensions of an unsatisfactory structure. By this time publishing had become the principal source both of revenue and of expenditure, surpassing printing. One can imagine a ghostly figure from the Printing House staff of Clay's and Wright's time saying that at last it had happened – the publishing gamble was dragging down the whole Press. But printing was facing its own difficulties: the Monotype era was over and new technologies, especially computer-operated setting, had to be accepted, with consequent capital expenditure in a market which was no more positive than publishing. And the fundamental structural weaknesses emerged: publishing was split between London and Cambridge, with an 'us and them' departmental jealousy. At long last the tension between the heads of the two divisions, printing and publishing, was forced into prominence. One was Secretary to the Syndicate, but did that make him more than just the head of the publishing business?

In 1970 Richard David formally vacated the Secretaryship, which was for the moment taken by the University Treasurer, Trevor Gardner, *ex officio* a Syndic. David took the title of Publisher, as head of the publishing business. In 1971 Lord Todd, Master of Christ's, became Chairman of the Press Syndicate, providentially, and he and the University Treasurer set about the reorganisation of the Press. They moved rapidly; they had to. In November of 1971 Todd made a report to the Syndicate outlining a plan; on 21 December

Geoffrey Cass was appointed Managing Director of the Publishing business, and he took office on 1 January 1972.

With equal speed he moved into action. Fortunately, he knew a good deal about the Press, having acted as management consultant a few years before. He had gone on to reorganise Allen and Unwin at the request of Sir Stanley Unwin and had become Managing Director there. At the Press some things had to be done immediately: the negotiation of an even larger overdraft to tide the Press through its restructuring; radical repricing of the back-list; very tight control of stocks and print-numbers; an embargo on new appointments. There were no dismissals of staff, who were not to be made responsible for the errors of management. Above all, there was no change of editorial policy: no restriction on the acceptance of new books, even the loss-makers. Cass recognised that it was the function of the Press to publish scholarly books, that the function could not be abdicated, even in a crisis, and that this part of the business was going well: the Cambridge list was full of strengths. It was in any case his strategy to move out of the crisis by planned expansion, since contraction could only leave the Press weaker in a time of recession. His main operating tactic was the control of cash and its generation; there was no point in making an accounting 'profit' if you have no money in the bank, and then have to pay corporation tax on a purely notional figure. Over the next years he consistently build up the cash reserve. By 1973 the balance was positive and it then began to rise rapidly and continuously.

In September 1972 Cass became the first clearly recognised Chief Executive of the whole Press, above the two divisions, whose heads were now both responsible to him. This resolved the constitutional ambiguity which had lurked as a danger ever since Wright was made Secretary in 1891 while Clay was still Partner as well as Printer and Secretary. The years 1973 and 1974 were times of restructuring: an Operations Director, a Marketing Director and a new Managing Director were appointed in the Publishing Division and a Printer-Designate in the Printing Division. In 1974 Crutchley and David could both retire confident that the Press was now safely recovered and in good hands.

Not that the outside world was a safer place for publishers or printers. It was in 1975 that inflation reached twenty-five per cent. Cass was still determined to expand out of trouble, but to achieve real growth in a world of hyper-inflation is specially difficult. None the less, acceptances of new books began to rise with extraordinary speed – helped to some degree by the fact that for the moment other English publishers were abandoning scholarly publishing, so that the Press became the only haven for many projects, or even whole fields of study. All the same, print-numbers remorselessly dropped; if in the 1960s they had been higher than they had ever been, now they were lower. Libraries and academic purchasers, dependent as they had been since the 1960s on central funding, found they had little money for books once they had paid their expenses, and this was a world-wide phenomenon.

Cass's next step was to gain for the Press charitable relief from taxation. He was convinced, both on historical and on analytical grounds that it was anomalous that an integral arm of the University, itself a charity, and an arm which fulfilled one of the University's prime purposes, the advancement and dissemination of knowledge, which was constituted and run in such a way that since 1916 no outside person or body had taken or could take any form of profit or dividend out of the operation – it was anomalous that a body of such a charitable nature should pay tax on 'profits'. If the Press was now able to make a surplus on the year's trading, that surplus served two wholly charitable purposes. In the first place it financed the continuance and growth of the Press's altruistic operations. In the second place it went into the reserve which was being built up to secure the Press and its parent University against the kind of danger which had threatened the Press's very existence in 1970–2. In any recurrence, the University would be even less able to afford to rescue the Press, which had long ago become too big relative to its parent to be so rescuable, and which could not for constitutional reasons be taken over or sold. A financially secure University Press would always be able to serve and to help the University and its charitable purposes in a multitude of different ways. Moreover, as this history has shown, there were documents, from the Charter of 1534 onwards, which attested to a growing historical awareness of the evolving charitable cultural function of the Press within the University. It should be possible, in a careful, indeed a massive

The Edinburgh Building, 1980.
(a) Completion of the Edinburgh Building meant that the whole publishing
operation could now be housed on one site, in a building-complex which
combined editorial and production functions, accounting, order-processing,
a bulk warehouse and forward stock-handling. Transport was now by road,
and it was no longer necessary, indeed it was uneconomical,
to use a London office.

presentation of the case, to convince the authorities. So Cass
presented such a case, cheerfully threatening to overwhelm
the Inspectorate of Taxes with an avalanche of documents.
The case was accepted without a fight in November 1976.
It is hard to overestimate the importance of the decision,
especially at that time. Oxford University Press watched

(b) An interior view.

progress with interest, then sought and received a similar decision based on the Cambridge precedent.

The last piece dropped into place in 1980, when at last the Publishing Division was united on one site in Cambridge. The Edinburgh Building, financed from the Press's own funds, was put up on the Shaftesbury Road site, facing the University Printing House. It has its own large warehousing facility as well as an office building designed to house the specialist operations of publishing groups. Bentley House had been sold a year or two earlier, and for a short time various departments worked in hired accommodation round about the Pitt Building. When finally everyone was on one site in a modern building with modern services, the power of the whole organisation was released into its function. In 1981 the building was formally opened by HM The Queen,

95

accompanied by the Chancellor of the University, HRH The Duke of Edinburgh, who had consented to the naming of the building.

And as if to draw a line under this part of the story, in 1981 the Senate of the University accepted a new Statute J, which codifies the now understood nature, function and constitution of the Press. It too is given in an appendix to this booklet. It is a distillation of the understanding of the whole historical evolution which has taken place since 1534, of which the chief dates and events are the first Charter itself; the foundation of the Press on that Charter in 1583; the first publications in 1584; the first Bible in 1591; the second Charter of 1628; Bentley's innovations of 1696; the Almanac Duty Act of 1781; the Royal Commission of 1851; the Partnership of 1854; the appointment of Wright in 1891; the dissolution of the Partnership in 1916; the opening of the American office in 1931 and its transformation into the Branch in 1949; and then the extraordinary series of profound analyses and bold decisions carried out by Geoffrey Cass between 1972 and 1980: a radical reform which like all the best reforms went back to the sources, *ad fontes*, and redefined the Press by insisting on its true nature.

The Press today continues to grow in scale and scope. In 1990 it issued over 1,400 new publications and marketed this output to more than 150 countries throughout the world. The range of publishing now encompasses virtually every subject seriously studied in the English-speaking world. It

HM The Queen, accompanied by the Chancellor of the University, HRH
The Duke of Edinburgh, at the opening ceremony of the Edinburgh
Building, with Geoffrey Cass, Chief Executive of the Press, Dr T. M. (later
Sir Morris) Sugden, Master of Trinity Hall and Chairman of the Press
Syndicate, and Philip Allin, Managing Director of the Publishing Division
and later University Printer.

has further diversified in the last decade into reference
works, medical publishing, electronic media and video.
Increasingly, the Press seeks its authors and its markets
overseas, in North America especially, but also in continental
Europe, Japan and Australasia. But this great expansion,
which now makes the Press one of the largest academic

The Chief Executive of the Press, Geoffrey Cass, addressing the reception in the Rotunda of the British Embassy in Washington during the North American Branch's celebrations of the 400th Anniversary of Cambridge University Press's printing and publishing in 1984. Principal guests included the Foreign Secretary, the Rt Hon. Sir Geoffrey Howe, and the British Ambassador to Washington, His Excellency Sir Oliver Wright.

The Australian Headquarters of Cambridge University Press, opened in 1984, the Press's quatercentenary year, in Oakleigh, near Melbourne.

publishers in the world, remains an organic expansion, purposefully and directly related to the Press's statutory aims, and realised through a single, unitary printing and publishing organisation, with its physical and its constitutional centre in Cambridge.

As if to emphasise this historical link with the booktrades in the old city, the Press in 1992 occupied the bookshop site at 1 and 2 Trinity Street, turning it into a showroom and shop. This is the oldest bookshop site in Britain; books have been sold there since the sixteenth century, perhaps since 1505. It looks across the road to Great St Mary's, the University Church, where former Stationers and University Printers were churchwardens and were buried. In the other direction, it faces the Senate House and the Old Schools, the area where Siberch and Thomas Thomas had their printing houses. Browsers in the new Cambridge showroom can see the whole range of Cambridge books in a setting which is a visible testimony to the continuity of Cambridge printing and publishing.

SOME CAMBRIDGE BOOKS AND AUTHORS

An academic publisher tends naturally to produce books for writers who are well known to other experts in the field, and may today reach fame by getting Nobel prizes; but for the most part their names are not household ones. So, for instance Pierre de la Ramée, known internationally as Ramus, the Latinised form of his name, was not a popular writer and is today only known to historians. But his *Dialectica*, of which Thomas Thomas published an edition in 1584, was one of the most influential books of its time, studied by students and scholars throughout Europe for a century and more. In publishing it, Thomas was as it were stating a programme of modernist enlightenment.

However, Cambridge does have its share, and more, of famous names. For instance, the new king, James I, was in 1603 an object of more than usual curiosity; so his *A Prince's Looking-Glass*, which gave his views on kingship, was – in the year of his coronation – a highly topical book. And in the seventeenth century Cambridge (that 'nest of singing birds') produced so many great poets that it was natural that some of their work was printed at the local press. George Herbert's *The Temple* – one of the masterpieces of English poetry – was first published at the Press in 1633, as was Phineas Fletcher's less famous *The Purple Island*. The very next year the Press printed John Donne's *Six Sermons on Several Occasions*, as well as Richard Crashaw's volume of Latin Epigrams. In 1638 in a little volume of *Obsequies to the Memory of Mr Edward King* readers found the first printing of Milton's 'Lycidas' – Milton's celebrated lament for his dead friend. In 1639 Thomas Fuller published his *History of the Holy War*. In 1646 Francis Quarles gave the Press his *Judgement and Mercy*, and in 1647 Henry More his *Philosophical Poems*.

In 1649 the Press published an edition of William Harvey's epoch-making work on the circulation of the blood, and in

1660 Ray's 'Catalogue' of plants, in the Cambridge region. These works founded the scientific publishing of the University, just as in 1643 an important edition of the Venerable Bede's 'History of the English Church' founded research into historical texts, and in 1694 Barnes's edition of Euripides founded the tradition of classical textual editorship published at the Press. The editions of Horace, Vergil, Catullus, Tibullus and Propertius, published by Tonson and printed at the Press between 1699 and 1702, were followed by Bentley's own Horace, which was a remarkable edition by any standard.

As Newton is the greatest name in Cambridge, or indeed English, science, so the new edition in 1713 of the *Philosophiae naturalis principia mathematica* with Bentley as entrepreneur was a corresponding landmark. It also set a precedent for the titles of ambitious books two hundred years later (see below).

In 1716 the Press printed Sir Thomas Browne's *Christian Morals*; and in the 1750s a series of Seatonian prize poems by the visionary Christopher Smart.

At the beginning of the eighteenth century the largest scholarly work hitherto undertaken by the Press was the monumental Greek–Latin Lexicon of Suidas; balanced at the end of the century (1793) by a type-facsimile of the Codex Bezae – one of the earliest manuscripts of the Greek New Testament and one of the greatest treasures of the University Library.

In the early part of the nineteenth century the Press

published for the scientist-reformers of the University like Whewell and Sedgwick, and for the Liberal Anglicans Thirlwall, Grote and F. D. Maurice. But it was in the 1880s and after that scientific and scholarly publishing really took off. Clark Maxwell, Rayleigh, and Kelvin were the first generation; at the same time the Press was publishing Jebb and Verrall in the classics, the great ethnologist Robertson Smith, the legal historians Pollock and Maitland, and the Orientalists E. G. Browne and Nicholson. Perhaps the best known are the still-read F. W. Maitland, who was a Syndic, and the Regius Professor Lord Acton, who was the inventor and planner of the Cambridge Histories.

This heroic period carried over into the first years of this century. In 1903 the Press published both J. J. Thomson's *Conduction of Electricity through Gases* and G. E. Moore's *Principia Ethica*; in the next year Eddington, Whitehead and Jeans began the tradition which led on to Schrödinger, Gamow and others; Sherrington's *Man on His Nature* took the tradition into the life sciences. Jeffrey's *The Earth* (1924, 6th edition 1976) was called 'the geophysicist's Bible'. George Sturt's *The Wheelwright's Shop* (1923) inaugurated the whole tradition of reflective retrospect on the common life of the English countryman which became a vogue in later years. The Press published the first books by the art historian Nikolaus Pevsner. Sir Frederick Bartlett's *Remembering* (1932) is one of the classics of psychology; Michael Oakeshott's first book *Experience and its Modes* a classic of political thought. A. E. Housman published with the Press most of his editions of the Latin classics and his celebrated lecture on *The Name and Nature of Poetry*.

In 1940, during the Battle of Britain, the Press produced three great works of scholarship: Dom David Knowles's *Monastic Orders in England*, R. M. Jackson's *Machinery of Justice in England*, and *The Cambridge Bibliography of English Literature*. After the war, in 1951–4, there appeared the three volumes of Runciman's *History of the Crusades*, and in 1952 the standard *Flora of the British Isles* compiled by Clapham, Tutin, and Warburg. In the same year appeared the first volume of Darby's *Domesday Geography of England*. In 1954 appeared the first volume of Joseph Needham's truly monumental *Science and Civilisation in China*. In 1956, in *Documents in Mycenean Greek*, Michael Ventris and John Chadwick found the linguistic key to unlock the history of the Mycenean civilisation, by deciphering the language of the incised clay tablets and discovering it to be an archaic form of Greek. In 1959 C. P. Snow's lecture *The Two Cultures* became a best-seller, and ultimately provoked F. R. Leavis's rejoinder. Leavis himself became a Press author with the re-issue of *Scrutiny* in twenty volumes in 1963, followed by a posthumous volume of collected papers. In theology C. H. Dodd's great work on *The Fourth Gospel* was complemented by his own more popular books for laymen, which had a wide sale in Britain and the USA.

The Press's schoolbooks publishing has traditionally been strong in mathematics, building on the textbooks produced

at the beginning of the century by the Harrow schoolmasters
Godfrey and Siddons (most notably their *Elementary Geometry*
and their best-selling *Four-Figure Tables*); in 1964 the Press
published the first volume in the *School Mathematics Project*,
one of the most successful curriculum reform schemes ever
undertaken in Britain, which in its modern editions is
adopted by about two-thirds of the secondary schools in the
UK; that in turn has been followed by the *Cambridge Primary
Maths* course (from 1989). At the other end of the curriculum,
so to speak, the *Cambridge Latin Course* and the *Cambridge
Greek Course* have dominated in a similar way.

The rapidly expanding English Language Teaching Programme has produced several innovative and best-selling
titles, including Adrian Doff, Christopher Jones and Keith
Mitchell, *Meanings into Words* (1984) and Ray Murphy, *English
Grammar in Use* (1985). The *Cambridge English Course* by
Michael Swan and Catherine Walter (from 1984) has
established itself as one of the major courses for British
English throughout the world, and is now supplemented by
parallel courses on American English (*Interchange*, from 1990)
and Australian English (from 1991).

In recent decades the Press has published a series of major
scholarly editions: *The Mathematical Papers of Isaac Newton*
edited by D. T. Whiteside and others; *The Letters and Works
of D. H. Lawrence* edited by James T. Boulton and others;
The Collected Letters of Joseph Conrad edited by Frederick Karl

and Laurence Davies; *The Correspondence of Charles Darwin* edited by F. Burkhardt. These editions are monuments of modern literary and historical scholarship, but the authoritative texts they establish can also be used as the basis of a range of popular derivatives.

In the sciences there have been important biographies of Isaac Newton, by Richard Westfall; of Erwin Schrödinger, by Walter Moore; of Paul Dirac, by Helge Kragh; and of Kelvin, by C. W. Smith and M. N. Wise. There have been major textbooks such as K. Schmidt-Nielsen's *Animal Physiology*; Paul Horowitz and Winfield Hill on *The Art of Electronics*; William Press's *Numerical Recipes*; and advanced monographs from distinguished physicists such as Stephen Hawking, Richard Feynman and Steven Weinberg.

In the humanities and social sciences the Press has recently published such internationally pre-eminent figures as John Lyons in linguistics; Edmund Leach, Jack Goody and Stanley Tambiah in anthropology; W. G. Runciman in social theory; Geoffrey Elton, Moses Finley, Eric Hobsbawm and Richard Southern in history; Charles Taylor, John Searle, Richard Rorty, Quentin Skinner, Jon Elster and Bernard Williams in philosophy and intellectual history.

The fast-developing programme of reference publishing has included David Crystal's innovative *Cambridge Encyclopedia of Language* (1987), followed by his even more ambitious *Cambridge Encyclopedia* (1990). The programme of major Cambridge Histories has continued with *Latin America*, edited by Leslie Bethell; *India*, edited by Gordon

Johnson and others; *China*, edited by John Fairbank and Dennis Twitchett; *Japan*, edited by J. W. Hall and others; and *The Cambridge Ancient History*, New Edition, edited by John Boardman and others.

APPENDIX 1

THE LETTERS PATENT OF 1534, IN
ENGLISH TRANSLATION

Henry VIII, by the grace of God King of England and France,
Defender of the Faith, and Lord of Ireland, To all to whom these
present letters may come, greeting. Know ye that we of our special
grace, and by our certain knowledge and mere motion, have
granted and given licence, and by these presents grant and give
licence, for ourselves and our heirs, to our beloved in Christ the
Chancellor, Masters, and Scholars of our University of Cambridge,
That they and their successors for ever may, by their writings
under the seal of the Chancellor of the said University, from time
to time assign, appoint and in perpetuity have among them,
and perpetually remaining and dwelling within our aforesaid
University, Three Stationers and Printers or Sellers of Books,
both aliens born outside our obedience and natives born within
our obedience, having and holding houses both leased and owned.
These Stationers or Bookprinters, assigned in the aforesaid manner,
and any of them, shall have lawful and incontestable power to print
there all manner of books approved, or hereafter to be approved, by
the aforesaid Chancellor or his deputy and three doctors there; and
also to exhibit for sale, as well in the same University as elsewhere
in our realm, wherever they please, all such books and all other
books wherever printed, both within and outside our realm,
approved or to be approved (as aforesaid) by the said Chancellor or
his deputy and three doctors there. And that the same Stationers or
Printers born (as is aforesaid) outside our obedience, and every of

them, for as long as they dwell in the aforesaid University and occupy themselves in the aforesaid business, shall in all things and by everyone be reputed, taken and treated as our faithful subjects and lieges, and each of them shall be so reputed, taken and treated. And they shall be entitled to enjoy and use all and singular liberties, customs, laws and privileges, and each of them shall be so entitled, freely and quietly, such as any faithful subject and liege in any manner can use and enjoy. And they shall pay and render Lot and Scot, taxes, tallages, and all other customs and impositions none otherwise and in no other manner than our own faithful subjects and lieges pay and render to us; any statute, act, ordinance or provision made, published or provided in the contrary notwithstanding. Provided always, that the said Stationers or Printers so born (as is premised) outside our obedience shall pay to us all and all manner of customs, subsidies and other monies owing to us from time to time for their goods and merchandise to be exported from or imported into our realm, in such wise as aliens pay us and not otherwise. In testimony of which matter we have caused these our letters to be made patent. Witness myself, at Westminster, the 20th day of July, in the 26th year of our reign [1534].

APPENDIX 2

STATUTE J OF THE UNIVERSITY

1 There shall be in the University a University Press which shall be devoted to printing and publishing in the furtherance of the acquisition, advancement, conservation, and dissemination of knowledge in all subjects; to the advancement of education, religion, learning, and research; and to the advancement of literature and good letters.

2 The management of the finance, property, and affairs generally of the University Press shall be the responsibility of the Press Syndicate which shall exercise in relation thereto all the powers of the University except in so far as the Statutes and Ordinances expressly or by necessary implication provide otherwise. The Press Syndicate shall consist of the Vice-Chancellor (or his deputy) as Chairman, the Treasurer, and such number of members of the Senate appointed in such manner as shall be determined from time to time by Ordinance.

3 The Press Syndicate shall have power in the name of the University and for the purposes of the University Press to purchase, lease, retain, sell, or transfer property real or personal and to purchase, retain, sell, or transfer securities (which term shall include stocks, funds, and shares) of any description whether or not authorised by law for the investment of trust funds, and this power shall extend to the investment (including the variation of the investment) of all endowments or other funds of the University Press.

4 All income accruing to the University Press shall be credited to the accounts of the Press Syndicate and all University Press capital and income shall be controlled by the Press Syndicate and applied by them at their sole discretion for the purposes of the University Press.

5 The Press Syndicate shall have power to borrow money for the purposes of the University Press and to make the property or income of the University Press security for any loan, provided that

   (*a*) the Syndicate shall comply with any limitations that may be imposed from time to time by the Financial Board under Statute F, I, 8 on such power to borrow money, and

   (*b*) the terms of any loan so secured on the property or income of the University Press shall be in accordance with the Universities and Colleges Estates Acts 1925 and 1964, and shall be approved by the Treasurer on behalf of the Financial Board.

6 The Press Syndicate shall have power in the name of the University to engage persons for employment in the service of the University Press, determine their salaries and pensions, and prescribe the conditions of their service.

7 Persons holding certain posts in the University Press which have been specially designated under this section by the Council of the Senate on the recommendation of the Press Syndicate shall be treated as University officers for the purposes of Statute A, II, 3, Statute A, III, 3, Statute B, I, 1, Statute B, III, 6 and Statute K, 3 (*b*).

8 The accounts of the University Press shall be audited annually by one or more qualified accountants appointed by the Financial Board, which shall in every year appoint one or more members of the Board to examine these accounts,

confer with the Auditor or Auditors, and report to the Board.

9 There shall be a Press Seal, as a seal of the University to be used on the directions of the Press Syndicate in matters relating to the affairs of the University Press; but the existence of the Press Seal shall not invalidate the use in connexion with such matters of any other seal of the University. The University shall have power to make Ordinances concerning the custody and affixing of the Press Seal.

10 The Press Syndicate shall have power to delegate any of their powers under this Statute subject to any limitations imposed by Ordinance.

11 The term property of the University Press here and elsewhere in Statutes and Ordinances shall refer to property of the University held or used for the purposes of the University Press. In favour of any person having dealings with the University Press a certificate signed by the Treasurer that any particular property is the property of the University Press, or that any limitations on borrowing have been complied with, shall be conclusive.

12 The Press Syndicate shall make an Annual Report to the Council, which shall be published to the University either as a whole or in summary.

13 Notwithstanding the provisions of the foregoing sections, the Council of the Senate shall have power in circumstances which the Council deems to be exceptional, after consultation with the Financial Board, to discharge the Press Syndicate, and to assume full responsibility itself for the management of the Press for the time being. If the Council has occasion to exercise the powers available under this section, the Council shall make a full report to the University on the circumstances necessitating such action.

APPENDIX 3

UNIVERSITY PRINTERS, 1583–1992

1583	Thomas Thomas, M.A.	1705	Cornelius Crownfield
1588	John Legate	1730	William Fenner
?	John Porter (before 1593)	1730	Mary Fenner
			Thomas James
			John James
1606	Cantrell Legge	1740	Joseph Bentham
?	Thomas Brooke, M.A. (before 1608)	1758	John Baskerville
		1766	John Archdeacon
1622	Leonard Greene	1793	John Burges
1625	Thomas Buck, M.A.	1802	John Deighton
	John Buck, M.A.	1802	Richard Watts
1630	Francis Buck	1804	Andrew Wilson
1632	Roger Daniel	1809	John Smith
1650	John Legate the younger	1836	John William Parker
1655	John Field	1854	George Seeley
1669	Matthew Whinn	1854	Charles John Clay, M.A.
1669	John Hayes		
1680	John Peck, M.A.	1882	John Clay, M.A.
1682	Hugh Martin, M.A.	1886	Charles Felix Clay, M.A.
1683	James Jackson, M.D.		
1686	Jonathan Pindar	1916	James Bennet Peace, M.A.
1693	H. Jenkes		
1697	Jonathan Pindar	1923	Walter Lewis, M.A.
		1945	Brooke Crutchley, M.A.

1974 Euan Phillips, M.A.

1976 Harris Myers, M.A.

1982 Geoffrey Cass, M.A.

1983 Philip Allin, M.A.

1991 Geoffrey Cass, M.A.

In 1991 the title of University Printer was combined with that of Chief Executive of the Press, reverting to the original historic position where the University Printer was the operational head of the whole Press.

APPENDIX 4

Charles John Clay   1874–93

R. T. Wright   1892–1911

A. R. Waller   1911–22

S. C. Roberts   1922–48

R. J. L. Kingsford   1948–63

R. W. David   1963–70

Trevor Gardner   1970–4

Geoffrey Cass, Chief Executive 1972, Secretary 1974–